The MAY DAYS Dialogues

A Series of Dramatic Dialogues

Eastern Promises	*Antoni Libera*
How Now Green Cow	*Julie Burchill*
The Wall-Dog	*Manfred Karge*
Disneyland It Ain't	*Sue Townsend*
True Love Stories	*Harwant S. Bains*
Goodnight Siobhan	*Jeananne Crowley*

The Royal Court Writers Series published by Methuen Drama
in association with the Royal Court Theatre

Royal Court Writers Series

The May Days Dialogues: this collection first published in Great Britain in the Royal Court Writers Series in 1990 by Methuen Drama, Michelin House, 81 Fulham Road, London SW3 6RB in association with the Royal Court Theatre, Sloane Square, London SW1N 8AS and distributed in the United States of America by HEB Inc., 361 Hanover Street, Portsmouth, New Hampshire 03801.

A CIP catalogue record for this book is available from the British Library.

ISBN 0-413-64700-5

Printed in England by Clays Ltd, St Ives plc

THE ENGLISH STAGE COMPANY
AT THE
ROYAL COURT

The history of the English Stage Company is generally held to have begun with the seminal production of John Osborne's LOOK BACK IN ANGER in May 1956. Since then, the Royal Court has consistently been the flagship of new writing and the principal home of the theatrical avant garde in this country.

First and foremost a theatre of new writing, the aim of the English Stage Company is to develop and produce the best in new writing for the theatre, encouraging writers from all sections of society to address the problems of our times. Early Court writers included: John Osborne, Arnold Wesker, John Arden, David Storey, Ann Jellicoe and Edward Bond. They were followed by a generation of writers led by David Hare and Howard Brenton and, in more recent years, the celebrated house writers have included Caryl Churchill, Timberlake Wertenbaker and Robert Holman.

In line with the policy of nurturing new writing, the Theatre Upstairs has mainly been seen as a place for exploration and experiment, where writers can hone their craft prior to the demands of the Mainstage auditorium. This has proved successful over the years and recent graduates to have moved from Upstairs to Down include Anne Devlin, Andrea Dunbar, Sarah Daniels, Jim Cartwright, Clare McIntyre and Timberlake Wertenbaker. In recent years rehearsed readings and workshops have sometimes been used to start the collaboration between writer, director and actors at an earlier point. Plays like SERIOUS MONEY or OUR COUNTRY'S GOOD were both written following periods of workshop research.

But, despite recent box office successes such as TOP GIRLS, SERIOUS MONEY, ROAD, TOM AND VIV and OUR COUNTRY'S GOOD; the 80's have been a period of diminished productivity as funding levels generally have declined. In particular, the English Stage Company has been unable to gain any substantial support from our local authority, the Royal Borough of Kensington and Chelsea. Last year the Theatre Upstairs was closed for 8 months. However, the English Stage Company has just received a generous uplift from the Arts Council for the coming year and, in May, the Theatre Upstairs re-opened for a season of work. Despite this encouragement, as the English Stage Company moves into the 1990's, it is alarmingly clear that the business of promoting new writing in the theatre is as precarious as ever. It is this knowledge coupled with commitment that gives the Royal Court a certain edge. And, as always, it is a mixture of idealism and pragmatism that will ensure the survival of the English Stage Company.

THE MAY DAYS
AN INTRODUCTION

As we moved into the 90's, theatre critics looked back on the 80's with dissatisfaction. They felt it had failed in some way. *"In the last decade, British Theatre has become less responsive to public events"* Michael Billington wrote in the Guardian (17.2.90). This feeling was echoed by Malcolm Bradbury in the Listener (15.2.90): *"In the 80's, theatre grew generally less political as subsidy gave way to sponsorship, agitprop to special effects"*.

I don't entirely accept the Bradbury/Billington axis: indeed the decade saw much of the fringe work of the 70's graduating to the stages of major theatres. Both a larger and a wider audience saw more plays with a political purpose than ever before. And, to take a broader view, the comparative vigour of British theatre since 1956 has been its ability to play a critical part in social debate. It has shown that it can be a third chamber: a fourth estate. It has demonstrated an agility and remarkable flexibility in approaching subjects as theatrically unpromising as the money markets or the housing boom. At the same time, the swift course of events in Eastern Europe at the end of 1989 and the end of a decade of Thatcherism here in Britain prompted a wish for a kind of *"Royal Court Instant Response Unit"*, able to give a theatrical platform to the immediate debate of political issues. In January 1990 we approached a number of writers who between them hold a wide range of political opinions. We invited them to write a 30 minute argument, in dialogue form, on a subject close to their hearts. Several took Eastern Europe as their theme, while other writers have chosen to focus on subjects as different as Irish determination for a United Ireland, Britain's current immigration policies and the theatre's trivialisation of the Aids debate.

The May Days season will stage 15 of these dialogues. Some will be rehearsed readings and some will be fully produced. There will be early evening and late night dialogues in the Theatre Upstairs at 7pm and at 10.30pm respectively and a bill of 3 dialogues will be in the Main Theatre each evening at 8pm.

Perhaps the difference between political theatre now and in the 70's, is that the answers are less immediately apparent. It is by giving audiences the opportunity to hear such cosmopolitan and diverse opinions that we hope to offer them a glimpse of political and social possibilities for the future.

M.S.C.
22 May 1990

MAY DAYS DIALOGUES - A SUMMARY

TRUE LOVE STORIES by Harwant S. Bains
Dipti Pankanya is a British citizen, but her liberties are threatened by her recent marriage. Harwant Bains is a young Asian writer whose plays include *Fighting Kite* for Stratford East and *Blood* for the Royal Court Theatre Upstairs.

HOW NOW GREEN COW by Julie Burchill
Julie Burchill, radical author and columnist asks: are Green issues simply moral cowardice masquerading as social conscience?

GOODNIGHT SIOBHAN
by Jeananne Crowley with Eamon Dunphy
The Northern Ireland conflict threatens to come between a couple for whom it might have been a night to remember. Jeananne Crowley is an Irish actress and writer.

CUTTING ROOM by Mark Fisher MP
Is censorship always wrong? A TV writer and his producer argue the true value of free speech. Mark Fisher is MP for Stoke-on-Trent Central and is Shadow Minister for Arts and Media.

THE SERPENT by Horia Girbea
The young Romanian playwright examines both communism and the current regime in the light of recent upheavals. Have things really changed?

THE LITTLE RABBI by David Hart
David Hart, novelist and libertarian political commentator, argues that all governments are ultimately prepared to use force to promote the interests of the state. Here, Stalin tries to justify his widespread use of violence against his people.

AIDS MEMOIR
by Nicholas de Jongh
The Guardian arts reporter and theatre critic asks whether the theatre has failed to recognise AIDS as a grave international emergency.

ACCOUNTING FOR THE FUTURE
by David Jenkins, The Bishop of Durham
How can we care about people and preserve the earth? Together, Adam and his uncle, Smith, face the need for a new approach to wealth.

THE WALL-DOG by Manfred Karge
Translated by Jane and Howard Brenton
An East German border guard and his dog face unemployment together. Manfred Karge is a German playwright, director and actor whose work is performed worldwide.

EASTERN PROMISES by Antoni Libera
Translated by Antonia Lloyd-Jones
Antoni Libera, Polish critic, writer and director asks: has Russia really changed? Is there any substance to Eastern promises?

TOMORROW by Doug Lucie
Playwright Doug Lucie tackles the thorny issue of arts sponsorship. A theatre director finds himself at the mercy of an old university contemporary, now an Arts Sponsorship Consultant

HINDSIGHT by Sheila Rowbotham
Late at night, a TV documentary editor is visited by the legendary Russian revolutionary leader, Alexander Kollontai. Sheila Rowbotham is a socialist, feminist writer and a freelance teacher and researcher.

XANTHIPPE'S REPUBLIC by Roger Scruton
Socrates comes home to his truculent wife after a hard day in the market place. A domestic quarrel turns into a philosophical debate. Roger Scruton is a philosopher and writer.

DISNEYLAND IT AIN'T by Sue Townsend
Who can cure the N.H.S? Maureen takes her dying daughter to Florida to meet Mister Mouse. Sue Townsend is a writer and novelist: best known for 'The Diary of Adrian Mole'.

KNIGHTLEY'S STATE by Fay Weldon
In the absence of any moral guidance from church or state, it is left to the writer to provide this leadership. A nobel prize-winning author outlines his vision of the future. Fay Weldon is a novelist, playwright and critic whose work is translated into many languages.

THE MAY DAY DIALOGUES

PRODUCTION

DESIGNER	**Peter Hartwell**
COSTUME DESIGNER	**Jennifer Cook**
LIGHTING DESIGNER	**Christopher Toulmin**
SOUND DESIGNER	**Bryan Bowen**
MUSIC (for *The Wall-Dog*)	**Orlando Gough**
CHOREOGRAPHY (for *The Wall-Dog*)	**Jane Anthony**
COSTUME SUPERVISOR	**Iona Kenrick**
ASSISTANT DIRECTOR	**Anna Birch**
STAGE MANAGER	**Neil O'Malley**
DEPUTY STAGE MANAGERS	**Gary Crant, Nicole Griffiths, Mark Ormerod, Katie Bligh**

Wardrobe care by PERSIL and COMFORT. Adhesive by COPYDEX and EVODE LTD. Ioniser for the lighting control room by THE LONDON IONISER CENTRE (836 0211). Cordless drill by MAKITA ELECTRIC (UK) LTD. Watches by THE TIMEX CORPORATION. Batteries by EVER READY. Refrigerators by ELECTROLUX and PHILIPS MAJOR APPLIANCES LTD. Microwave by TOSHIBA UK LTD. Kettles for rehearsals by MORPHY RICHARDS. Video for casting purposes by HITACHI. Coffee machines by CONA. Microwave for backstage use kindly supplied by ELECTROLUX. Freezer for backstage use supplied by ZANUSSI LTD "Now that's a good idea".

With thanks to the British Council and Visiting Arts for their assistance.

FUNDED BY
THE ROYAL BOROUGH OF
KENSINGTON & CHELSEA

Funded by

LONDON BOROUGHS GRANTS SCHEME

PHONE NOW NO BOOKING FEE
FIRST CALL
01-836 2428
24HR CREDIT CARD SERVICE

FINANCIALLY ASSISTED BY GLA

Recipient of an Arts Council Incentive Funding Award

THE OLIVIER APPEAL

The Royal Court Theatre was very proud of Lord Olivier's patronage of our Appeal. It will continue in his name as a memorial to his life and talent.

The Appeal was launched in June 1988 - the Royal Court's 100th anniversary year. The Target is £800,000 to repair and refurbish the theatre and to enable the English Stage Company to maintain and continue its worldwide reputation as Britain's "National Theatre of New Writing".

The Royal Court would like to thank the following for their generous contributions to the Appeal:

Abbey Life
Adwest Group plc
Edgar Astaire
The Hon. M.L.Astor's 1969 Charitable Trust
Associated British Foods
Sir Richard Attenborough
Andrew Bainbridge
The Clifford Barclay Trust
Olivier Berggruen
Phyllis Blackburn
The Elaine and Neville Blond Charitable Trust
Paul Brooke
Christopher Campbell
Carole Catto
Isador Caplan
Peter Carter
The John S.Cohen Foundation
The Cowdray Trust
Graham Cowley
D'Oyley Carte Charitable Trust
David Croser
The Douglas Heath Eves Trust
Douglas Fairbanks
The Economist
Mr and Mrs Nicholas Egon
The Esmee Fairbairn Trust
Esselte Letraser
Matthew Evans

Evans and Reiss
Robert Flemming & Company
Brian Friel
Michael Frayn
Gala (100th Anniversary)
Collette Gleeson
The Goodinton Trust
Lord Goodman
Roger Graef
Christopher Hampton
Hatter (IMO) Foundation
The Hedely Trust
Anthony and Jennifer Hopkins
Claude Hug
Mrs P.P. Hyde
The Inchape Charitable Trust Fund
Jacobs Island Co plc
The John Lewis Partnership
Bernard Krichefski
Parry Kershaw Ltd
The Kobler Trust
Eddie Kulukundis
The London and Edinburgh Trust
The Mercers
Midgley Snelling and Co
Richard Mills
Portia Mores
Anna Louise Neuberg Trust
Richard Nickols
Olivier Banquet

A.J.G Patenall
Peter Jones
Pirelli Ltd
Irene Pruller-Daff
A.J.R.Purssell
Mr and Mrs J.A.Pye's Charitable Settlement
St Quentin Ltd
The Rayne Foundation
Lady Richardson
Mrs Ruth Rogers
R.S.Rubin
The Lord Sainsbury Trust
Andrew Sinclair
Wing Commander and Mrs Sinclair
1964 Charitable Trust
W.H.Smith & Son
The Spencer-Wills Trust
Max Stafford-Clark
Louise Stein
"Stormy Monday" Charity Premiere
Angela Thorne
Mary Trevelyan
Tracey Ullman
Andrew Wadsworth
Timothy West and Prunella Scales
Anthony Wilson
Women's Playhouse Trust
Irene Worth
Sandra Yarwood

THE ROYAL COURT THEATRE SOCIETY

For many years now Members of the Royal Court Theatre Society have received special notice of new productions, but why not become a Friend, Associate or a Patron of the Royal Court, thereby involving yourself directly in maintaining the high standard and unique quality of Royal Court productions - while enjoying complimentary tickets to the shows themselves?

Subscriptions run for one year; to become a Member costs £12, a Friend £60 (joint) £40 (single), an Associate £400, a Patron £1,000.

PATRONS Jeffrey Archer, Diana Bliss, Issac Davidov, Alfred Davis, Mr & Mrs Nicholas Egon, Mrs Henny Gestetner, Lady Eileen Joseph, Stonewall Productions Ltd., Tracey Ullman, Timberlake Wertenbaker, Irene Worth.

ASSOCIATES David Capelli, Michael Codron, Jeremy Conway, London Arts Discovery Tours, Patricia Marmont, Nick Hern Books, Greville Poke, Jane Rayne.

FRIENDS Paul Adams, S.M.Alexander, Roger Allam & Susan Todd, Jane Annakin, John Arthur, Francis & Cherry Baden-Powell, Mrs M.Bagust, Veronica Ball, Dee Barnfield, Linda Bassett, Paul Bater, Richard Baylis, A. Bingley Wright, Mr P.Binning & Ms A.Fulton, Anthony Blond, Brian Boylan, Irving H.Brecker, Alan Brodie, Stuart Burge, Max Burton, Peter Burtt-Jones, Kevin Byrne, Neil Goodhue Cady, Laurence Cann, Annie Castledine, Ben Chamberlain, Guy Chapman, Steve Childs, Lee Collier, Sandra Cook, Lou Coulson, Harriet Cruickshank, B.R.Cuzner, I.Dallaway, Mrs Der Pao Graham, Cathy Dodgeon, Julia Dos Santos, R.H. & B.H.Dowler, Adrian Charles Dunbar, Pamela Edwardes, C.Elliott, George A.Elliott III, Gillian Emmett, Patricia England, Kenneth Ewing, Sandra Eyre, Kate Feast, Leonard Fenton, Mr & Mrs Thomas Fenton, Robert Fox, Gilly Fraser, Dr Robert Galvin, David Gant, Kerry Gardner, Sarah Garner, Anne Garwood, Alfred Molina & Jill Gascoine, Timothy Gee, B.H. Geismar, Frank & Woji Gero, Ronald Gidseg, Miriam Gilbert, Janet and Michael Gill, Lord Goodman, A.C.Gorva, I.Gray Esq, Rod Hall, Lorraine Hamilton, Sharon Hamper, David Hardy and Sue Hillwood Harris, Shahab Hanif, Rosemary Hanson, J.H.Hards, A.M.Harrison, Vivien Heilbron, Sarah Hellings, Ashley & Pauline Hill, Ms Signe Loffos, Angus Hone, Maureen Hope Wynne, David Horovitch, Jack Howard, Susan J.Hoyle, Nigel P.Hudson, Diana Hull, Susan Imhof, Trevor Ingman, Kenny Ireland, Jonathan Isaacs, Richard Jackson, Dick Jarrett, Hugh Jenkins, Rowland Jobson, Donald Jones, Dr & Mrs David Josefowitz, Andrew Joseph, Annely Juda, Mark Knox, Mrs O.Lahr, Duncan Lamb, Dr R.J.Lande, Peter Leadill, C.C.Lee, Sheila Lemon, Peter L.Levy, Tony and Julia Ling, Robert S.Linton, John & Erica Macdonald, Mr & Mrs Roger Mace, Dr Anne Mackie, Paul Mari, Pete Maric, Marina Martin, Patricia Marx, S.A.Mason, Paul Matthews, Elaine Maycock, Philip L.McDonald, James Midgley, Anthony Minghella, Mimi Morris, Mr G. F.Mulhern, T. Murnaghan, R Murphy and S Deeks, Rosy Nasreen & Dr Conal Liam Mannion, Linda Newns, Sally Newton, Miss W.G.North, Michael Nyman, Catherine O'Brien, Richard O'Brien, Eileen & John O'Keefe, Elizabeth and Paul O'Shea, Stephen Oliver, Gary Olsen, Mark Padmore, Norman Papp, Clare and Oliver Parker, Alan David & Jane Penrose, Pamela Percy, Pauline Pinder, Harold Pinter, Nigel Planer, Laura Plumb, Adam Pollock, Dr A.G.Poulsen Hansen, Trevor Preston, Dr G.Pullen and Mrs P.Black, R.Puttick, Margaret Ramsay, Alex Renton, B.J. & Rosmarie Reynolds, E.W.Richards, Alan Rickman, Martin & Jennifer Roddy, Anton and Elizabeth Rodgers, R.S.Rubin, Christie Ryan, Jeremy and Nora Sayers, George Schneider, Leah Schmidt, Julia Scott, Rosemary Squire, Martin & Glynis Scurr, Jennifer Sebag-Montefiore, Mrs L.M.Sieff, Paul Sinclair Brooke, Peter A.Smith, Ms Caroline Staunton, Louise Stein, Richard Stokes, Richard Stone, Geoffrey Strachan, Rob Sutherland, Dudley Sutton, K & A Sydow, Nigel Terry, Amanda and R.L.W.Triggs, Elizabeth Troop, E.B.A.Truter, Eirlys Tynan, Kiomars Vejdani, Karen and Wes Wadman, Andrew Wadsworth, Harriet Walter, Tim Watson, Mrs B.E.Woollatt, Nicholas Wright, Charles and Victoria Wright, Peter B. Young, Silke Ziehle.

FOR THE ROYAL COURT

DIRECTION

Artistic Director	Max Stafford-Clark
Deputy Director	Jules Wright
Associate Director	Lindsay Posner
Casting Director	Lisa Makin
Acting Literary Manager	Melanie Kenyon
Artistic Assistant	Helen Carter
Arts Council Writer In Residence	Clare McIntyre
Resident Playwright	Victoria Hardie
Gerald Chapman Award Trainee Director	Anna Birch

PRODUCTION

Production Manager	Bo Barton
Master Carpenter	Chris Bagust
Deputy Master Carpenter	John Stritch
Chief Electrician	Johanna Town
Deputy Chief Electrician	Les Lyon
Electrician	Denis O'Hare*
Trainee Electrician	Mattea Godstein
Sound Designer	Bryan Bowen
Board Operators	Jonquil Pantin*
	Steve Hepworth*
Wardrobe Supervisor	Jennifer Cook
Acting Deputy Wardrobe Supervision	Iona Kenrick
Wardrobe Trainee	Karen Newman

ADMINISTRATION

General Manager	Graham Cowley
Assistant to General Manager	Georgia Cheales
Finance Administrator	Mark Rubinstein
Finance Assistant	Rachel Harrison
Press (730 2652)	Tamsin Thomas
Marketing and Publicity Manager	Guy Chapman
Development Manager	Anne-Marie Thompson
Development Assistant	Nina Dawson
House Manager	Gambol Parker
Deputy House Manager	Alison Smith
Box Office Manager	Gill Russell
Box Office Assistants	Gerald Brooking, Rita Sharma
Stage Door/Telephonists	Michele Baker* Jan Noyce*
Evening Stage Door	Tyrone Lucas*
Maintenance	John Lorrigio*
Cleaners	Eileen Chapman* Ivy Jones*
Fireman	Paul Kleinmann*

YOUNG PEOPLE'S THEATRE

Director	Elyse Dodgson
Administrator	Dominic Tickell
Youth and Community Worker	Euton Daly

* Part-time staff

COUNCIL:

Chairman: John Mortimer, Chris Bagust, Bo Barton, Stuart Burge, Anthony C.Burton, Harriet Cruickshank, Simon Curtis, Allan Davis, David Lloyd Davis, Elyse Dodgson, Robert Fox, Jocelyn Herbert, Hanif Kureishi, Sonia Melchett, James Midgley, Joan Plowright CBE, Greville Poke, Richard Pulford, Jane Rayne, Jim Tanner, Sir Hugh Willatt.

This theatre is associated with the Thames Television Theatre Writer's Scheme.

Eastern Promises

Antoni Libera

translated by Antonia Lloyd-Jones

Eastern Promises was first performed at the Royal Court on 7 June 1990 with the following cast:

Phil	Nicholas le Prevost
Phob	Richard Wilson

Directed by Kenny Ireland

Phil *an idealist, optimist and general enthusiast; he is dressed in corduroy trousers, a loose, comfortable sweater, suede shoes and a scarf.*

Phob *a realist, pessimist and general malcontent; he is dressed in a bow-tie, tweed jacket, dark trousers and brogues. He carries a walking stick and wears a signet ring.*

Phil *and* **Phob** *are sitting on a park bench, each reading a copy of the same newspaper, called* New Europe.

Phil's *face is the picture of cheerfulness and downright joy at life; now and then he puts on a positive expression or makes an affirmative gesture.*

Phob's *face is the picture of disquiet and irritation; now and then he puts on a resentful expression or makes a dismissive gesture.*

Phil (*following Phob's latest, particularly noticeable outburst of spleen*) Excuse me for asking, but what are you so upset about?

Phob Oh, it's not even worth talking about!

Phil We're reading the same paper, and unless I'm very much mistaken, we're reading exactly the same article, so forgive me for being so direct, but I can't help wondering what you're so annoyed about.

Phob The whole damned thing, I tell you, the whole damned thing, I say!

Phil (*dismayed*) Steady on a moment – let me just make sure: is that how you feel about the article called 'Eastern Europe Awakes', the article . . .

Phob (*impatiently*) Yes.

Phil . . . about the collapse of communism . . .

Phob Yes indeed!

Phil . . . and about the new order that's arisen as a consequence?

Phob Yes, that's the one.

Phil (*standing up*) Allow me to introduce myself: my name is Phil, I work for the Foundation for European Reunity.

Phob Oh yes, I've heard of it – they call it 'FOUNDER', don't they?

Phil Do they? Oh.

Phob Anyway, pleased to meet you. My name is Phob. I don't work for anyone, except myself.

Phil I'm intrigued by your views – are you a communist perhaps?

Phob Me? A Communist? That's a fine one!

Phil I just don't understand you then. How can you be so upset about the collapse of communism?

Phob Who told you communism has collapsed?

Phil What an extraordinary thing to say! Solidarity's in power in Poland, Vaclav Havel's President of Czechoslovakia, that tyrant Ceausescu's been shot, they've demolished the Berlin Wall and Honecker's under house arrest. And you're trying to tell me communism hasn't collapsed!

Phob I think you're being awfully naive. The truth is quite different. Not a single one of the East European countries has *formally* done away with communism. Not one of them has *officially* renounced Marxism-Leninism as the state ideology. All right, I admit they've stopped talking about it, they've stopped quoting it, and they've even allowed it to be criticized. But that's not the same as wiping it out, radically obliterating it for once and for all. And anyway, the most crucial point is that communism hasn't even budged an inch in Russia.

Phil They've removed the article about the leading role of the Communist Party from the Soviet Constitution, they've made economic advances towards a market economy, they're opening up towards the West and they've a free flow of information – does all that mean nothing to you?

Phob My dear fellow, you're letting yourself be taken in! It's all just a game, a great, big game, a colossal masquerade designed for people as naive as yourself. Those are just new, more effective political means, but the basic aims of that empire haven't changed at all. What do you think this lively scientific and cultural exchange that's going on with Russia nowadays is really all about? I suppose you think we're going to learn something from them? What a joke! Its sole purpose is for Russia to get its hands on modern technology for nothing. All those high-flown conferences, seminars and meetings always come to the same thing: we end up sending goods to Russia, and them money to pay for them. In some ways the situation's even more threatening than it was before.

Phil Excuse me for saying so, but you seem to be a bit of a doctrinarian. You've got a set pattern of thinking and you're applying it to reality, and if the facts just happen to run against the grain, then that's just too bad for the facts. You're not in the least bit interested in what's going on around you, you're only interested in your own way of looking at things, you'd do anything to protect it, you're twisting the facts to a point of absurdity.

Phob Well, I say you don't understand the basic point of these facts. (*In a schoolmasterly tone.*) It is Russia's intention to swallow us whole! Russia's real plan is to engulf the whole of Europe!

Phil Oh very funny! That's the first time I've heard of any country – and a superpower at that – setting out on schemes for expansion by relaxing its foreign policy and releasing subservient nations from its grip.

Phob I can see you don't play chess.

Phil I do, of course I do.

Phob Then you ought to know what a gambit is.

Phil Yes, it's when you sacrifice a piece in order to gain a strategic advantage.

Phob Right.

Phil Ah, so you think releasing the East Europeans from their power, withdrawing troops and giving up control of the security services there is just such a gambit? What on earth can you imagine they'll do as a follow-on attack?

Phob I'll tell you exactly what they'll do. All those East European countries – as Russia jolly well knows – have no greater dream than to join up with the West, to 'return to Europe', as they put it nowadays. And the West is coming out to meet them half-way. They're starting to pump a massive amount of capital into the East. And that's the *real* point! If you can't beat the West by military force, you've got to do it by economic force! If Mahommed won't come to the mountain, you've got to get the mountain to go to Mahommed! And that's exactly what Russia's attack will be!

Phil You're turning the whole thing back to front. Maybe what you've described *is* an attack, but it's the West that's doing the attacking, and not the East at all. Pumping capital into the East isn't charity, quite the opposite – it's the way to capture that market, make colossal profits and broaden the sphere of Western civilization. Who do you think's coming under whose thumb in this game?

Phob Hold on a minute! Of course, for a while the West *will* make some profit in the East, but one fine day those countries, with Russia in their wake, will be more or less back on their feet, and then the tables will suddenly turn. Do you know what the NEP was? (**Phil** *starts to answer, but* **Phob** *doesn't let him get a word in edgeways.*) You don't. So listen then . . .

Phil The New Economic Policy, brought in by Lenin in 1921, after four years of so-called 'war communism' . . .

Phob . . . which had brought the young Soviet state to the brink of utter ruin . . .

Phil It was a quasi-capitalist policy which . . .

Phob . . . once it had stood the country back on its feet, was immediately done away with by Stalin. In a nutshell, what they're up to now is really just an NEP, but on a massive, international scale. Their only aim is to build up strength, and then they'll push the limits of their influence forward once again, even further west this time. I can't just sit back and calmly watch as we let ourselves be duped! It's just the classic bait: all this liberalization, all this democratization is nothing but a tasty scrap of cheese, as fresh as fresh can be, temptingly set beneath the jaws of a lethal mousetrap!

Phil If you really want to convince me, you'll have to support your argument with some facts!

Phob OK, consider the basic facts. If you take Eastern Europe and the European part of Russia, that covers well over half the territory of our entire continent. It's the same in terms of population. When it comes to civilization, the West is highly advanced, and it's democratic; the East is backward, deep in debt, and either it's had the idea of democracy knocked out of it at root level, or else it's entirely ignorant of it. Do you really think such an imbalance can bode well for us? (**Phil** *wants to say something, but* **Phob** *doesn't let him interrupt.*) As an economic system, communism's bankrupt. And they're aware of that. And now they want to get themselves out of it. They want to get civilized at any cost. But how on earth can they do it, when they're at least fifty, if not a hundred years behind? Everything's crumbling so fast around them they don't even know where to start, what to grab hold of first. So we're their only hope. Without us they can't move an inch. They desperately need our technology, our immediate help with the food supply. So quick as a flash they've given birth to a brand new doctrine, and they're busy promoting it. 'A united Europe, free of conflict? Just what the West has always wanted! But on one condition only: that we come along with you. Or else there won't be peace. We must do away with partitions, we must live in a spirit of friendship. Of course, we're not free of blame,' they say, 'we admit that thanks to the blunders of Stalin, Khrushchev and Brezhnev a lot of bad things happened. But we freely admit it, if you please, and we're resigning for once and for all from our inglorious past. Now we're declaring *glasnost* and *perestroika*, freedom and pluralism. But . . . but we do expect reciprocation.' And the West is buying it. After almost fifty years of living in fear of the Soviet beast they're sighing with relief. 'At last! At last the threat is over, we'll trade, do business.' But my reply to that is: 'Watch out! Come to your senses quickly! You won't even notice when they get the upper hand and start laying down the law.' Can you really imagine a united Europe, entirely free of conflict, with Russia in on it?

Phil You're making Russia into the devil incarnate! But you're ignoring a most essential point – by letting us into their lives they're letting themselves, in a sense, be subordinated, and that means renouncing their own aggression and piracy.

Phob That's the way it looks, up to a point. Until one fine day they get out of their depression and stop being so happy to live under worse conditions than us. Really not even you can doubt that whatever we do for them, however well they turn out under our influence, they'll never catch us up – they'll just go on being left behind. The gap between us, in terms of civilization, could, at best, narrow a bit, but there's no way it can be closed up any more. The difference in standards nowadays isn't just the result of the last fifty or seventy years, it's the result of whole centuries. And that very difference was the essential reason – and it's still the essential reason why Russia's so unfriendly and hostile towards the West. And since there's no hope of those standards ever being on a par, there can never be any hope of getting rid of their hostile attitude. So however we help them, there's always going to come a day when they say it's all unfair – that we're rolling in it and that they're being taken for a ride. Then they'll demand more and more, they'll start demanding '*justice*'. But their idea of justice will only mean one thing: that we're obliged to keep them. (*Pause.*) Don't you see, if the only problem we had was those smaller countries that have come under Russia's influence, like Poland, Czechoslovakia, Hungary, and what have you, then maybe something would come of it – they'd be in no position to offer us a threat. But with Russia in the count the deal just won't work – it's just too powerful and random an element to let itself be brought to heel, as you seem to think it will. And those smaller countries – in spite of the nominal sovereignty and independence they've achieved – should still be treated with extreme caution, for the simple reason that they haven't yet managed to extract themselves irrevocably from under Russia's thumb – they should still be regarded as the outposts of an empire.

Phil This is a very jaundiced view of things. You totally fail to account, for example, for the effects of consumerism. There's nothing quite so pacifying as material comfort, even the very chance to achieve it, and the very pursuit of it. Just take a look around you. (*He gestures towards the auditorium.*) It's quite enough to teach them a few basic things, show them how to make money, and all the things they can get for it, and I promise you, they'll never have a second thought. All those military ideas, the constant need to be armed and ready for battle will leave their heads for ever. They'll be far too absorbed in getting rich, they'll be totally possessed by objects. And the more of them they pile up, the more sybaritic they'll become – they'll lose all desire for world conquest.

Phob Do you really think it's as simple as that? That it's enough to make formal changes to their system, and that'll just turn the whole situation about and start making profits straightaway? You're living in a dream world! You obviously don't understand the basics of communism. It's not just a flawed economic system allied to a police state. More than anything it's a machine for remodelling people – to ruin them, to make them react and behave in the exact opposite way to what we regard as right and natural. Communism, once activated, works in much the same way as a cancer cell in the human body. It doesn't only destroy healthy structures and social set-ups, it paralyses one's self-defence system, it gets to the 'immune system', as it were, until it reaches the point where a man who thinks he's acting in his own interest starts actually acting against himself. People who live in a reality permeated by communism gradually lose all sense of what's good for them and what is bad. The needles of their moral compass lose their magnetism. Their self-preservation instinct fades.

Phil All right, then how do you explain the succession of movements for freedom in the East European countries since the war? The Hungarian Uprising, the Prague Spring, the tireless unrest and rebellion in Poland, crowned at last by the emergence of Solidarity? According to your theory, those events could never have taken place. And yet they have.

Phob Not at all, I don't deny for a moment they were genuine. But that doesn't in the least invalidate my theory. I'm not talking about the brave heroic acts of exceptional individuals or daring public shows of strength that hit the headlines. In the every day struggle to survive Communism the main weapons are things like theft, shirking one's duties or falsifying the figures or telling lies in general. Do you realize what the long-term result of turning your values inside out like that can be?

Phil That's not an irreversible state of affairs. Man is capable of adapting quickly – you just have to show him that honesty and hard work have their rewards.

Phob It'd be a great mistake to think capitalism could be their salvation. It'll never save them, because they just aren't up to it. You've got to work hard under capitalism, you've got to show all-round initiative, you've got to keep on taking risks. Only then do you get any results, only then can you get rich, only then can you get hold of those enticing rewards of consumerism that you prescribe as their remedy. But what have you got over there? They're so fundamentally conditioned out of all these habits. They simply aren't capable of it. So how are they going to get out of this rut? And what if they don't – they'll just end up hating us all the more!

Phil What?! They're absolutely fascinated by us! They want to copy everything we do, even the things we do badly!

Phob They may be fascinated by us *now*! When they're right at the bottom of the heap. But give it a couple of years, and their enthusiastic tone will change into bitterness, disillusion and resentment. They'll look on us the way the Third World regards the United States, as even we regard them at times. Have you ever heard of the South Americans feeling any great admiration for the States? I certainly never have, I can tell you. Quite the contrary.

Phil Oh, but the United States is an entirely different thing – their expansionism is a sort of threat.

Phob Give it a couple of years, and that's just what Eastern Europe will be saying about us. And much louder at that, because we tower above them incomparably more than America does over the Third World.

Phil On the contrary, anyone even vaguely familiar with the history of

Poland, Hungary and Czechoslovakia, their national traditions and
character, will see at once that your thesis about their potential hatred of
the West is quite simply absurd. They are, and they always have been
particularly pro-Western, and anyway they're distinct for their peaceful
nature not for rapacious greed. Well maybe some people can't see any
virtue in that at all and criticize them for it as if it were a weakness, but
then that's another matter. Anyway, all their changes and revolutions are
for the most part entirely bloodless, or else have had very few victims
compared with what's happened and what's happening elsewhere in the
world. The Poles for instance don't even have a hostile attitude to the
Germans, who put them through massive suffering during the Second War.

Phob Either you don't understand what I'm saying, or else you're just
not listening. Did I mention the hostility of the Poles, the Czechs or the
Hungarians? What I'm talking about is the Soviet empire, and Russia as
its nucleus. All the other countries in Eastern Europe only enter into play
in as much as they're still within that superpower's sphere of influence.
There are two questions to be asked: firstly, have those countries really
disconnected themselves enough for us to look on them as truly separate
and individual? And secondly, is Russia really becoming a truly democratic
state, which you could fearlessly include as an equal partner in a unifying
Europe? Your answer to both these questions is yes, mine is no.

Phil I'm not so sure if our answers are the answers to such precisely
worded questions. I'm more under the impression they're responses to a
possible state of affairs, and not the actual one. You quite simply deny the
very possibility of change in that part of the continent, while I not only
don't exclude such a possibility, but am even prepared to state that at last
our chance has come to make it a reality. That's the essence of our
difference of opinion.

Phob You believe in the possibility of Russia transforming itself into a
democratic state? You believe one day they'll have a system more or less
like our own?

Phil And why ever not? If after something as monstrous as fascism the
Germans have managed to change out of all recognition, and in a very
short space of time at that, if a country as predatory and culturally alien
as Japan has undergone such advanced Europeanization, then why the
hell shouldn't Russia manage it?

Phob What a comparison! Just think what traditions of civilization they've
got in Germany and Japan, and what they've got in Russia! You've just

mentioned the two most resilient, industrious countries in the world! How on earth can you compare them with Russia?

Phil Very easily. Germany's social and economic depression after the First World War and Japan's great poverty after the Second were far deeper and more serious than Russia's present crisis. And just take a look at what they've got nowadays.

Phob It'll never be like that in Russia!

Phil You're digging your heels in like a child.

Phob Ah, you simply don't know history! You know nothing at all about that country!

Phil I'm sure you know far more than I do, but I don't think I can really learn anything from you. Your way of holding a discussion is mainly to give vent to your own prejudices.

Phob Prejudices?! They're not prejudices! (*In a schoolmasterly tone.*) Russia has always followed a different path from Europe. Russia never had the usual feudal system, it never had a Renaissance, it never produced a middle class, and it's never experienced capitalism in its standard form. Russia has never really emerged from a system of slavery. The concepts of Law, private ownership and freedom of the individual – key concepts in Western Europe – are virtually unheard of there. All land, the entire population and all their property have always belonged to the Absolute Ruler. This highly despotic system was their inheritance from the Mongols, who ruled them for centuries. The terrible cruelty of the Tartar yoke warped them for ever after. So now do you say I'm just mouthing prejudice?

Phil Have you really considered what the consequences of your outlook would be, if it were taken for real? You're saying, no more no less, that Russia is doomed: 'tainted', 'incurably sick', 'devoid of all hope of recovery'. Suppose you're right. And then what? What are you going to do about it? Destroy the place? Conquer, divide and rule it? That's pure childishness, not to say utter madness.

Phob You're being perverse! Have I been encouraging any sort of active response whatsoever? Isn't it perhaps the case that it's other people (*He shakes the newspaper.*) who are urging certain *actions*, people just like you – while all I've been doing is warning you against doing anything like that? Who's inciting who, is it you or me?

Phil Hold on a minute! Hold it right there! You can't weasel your way out of it like that! You said Russia, for such and such a reason, is corroded by evil, and with that evil it torments itself and everyone else around it; that it has an in-built, ceaseless desire for expansion, for preying on others; to put it in one, that Russia presents a massive threat for the rest of the world. All right. But can we really allow ourselves to sit back and let that conclusion rest? That would mean either we're denying our own fears, or else that we're meekly going to sign our own death warrant. So we have to take some sort of action. And that's why I think the most sensible thing we can do right now is to try and cure them – tame them, I mean, civilize them, help lift them out of their age-old decline. It's not just our duty as Europeans, it's also a vital chance for us.

Phob (*interrupting*) Our duty as Europeans is above all to protect and save ourselves! Since when, throughout history and politics, has altruism been a motive for a course of action? You're not just naive, you're also a hypocrite! Do you know what's behind your line of thought? Fear, that's all! You're quite simply petirifed of them, and that's what dictates your noble concepts! Your real understanding is this: they're savage, and they're stronger than us, so why get on the wrong side of them? Let's simply pay them off and have peace and quiet. We can afford it, after all. Why call the wolf out of the forest? Better to feed it up and spoil it a bit. I find that utterly sickening and idiotic all at once. It's sickening because it's a sheer indication of a loss of face, and it's idiotic because it only works in the very short term.

Phil (*sarcastically*) So you've never lost face, I suppose, have you? Tell me how you manage it.

Phob I haven't lost face, because I'll never agree to certain things.

Phil What things won't you agree to exactly?

Phob What I won't agree to is letting them get off lightly. I, as a true European, if you please, stand by the principle of Law. And it's a simple enough principle: if someone commits a crime, they can't escape retribution. That's what happened to the Germans. They committed crimes against humanity, and they paid dearly for it. They stood before the world's tribunal, and it passed judgement on them. But the Russians have led a life of crime for decades, if not centuries, yet they've never stood at the pillory. They've always got away with it and they're still getting away with it. Millions have been murdered, whole nations enslaved, nature destroyed and what is done about it? Nothing. 'Certain mistakes were made in the past,' they say. 'Evil came upon us from the West,' they say, 'communism was invented by a German Jew; it's the West that's responsible for all our misfortunes and diasters; Holy Russia is and always has been pure in essence, she will be the origin of the rebirth of humanity.' I've often heard that refrain. And I'll tell you straight – as long as the world refuses to stand up to them with a firm and decisive 'No!', any attempt to come to an understanding or a settlement with Russia will sooner or later result in a set-back for the West.

Phil So how do you imagine arranging this world tribunal over Russia? As far as I understand it, in order to pass judgement on someone, first you've got to bring them to court. Have you got that sort of power at your disposal? And even if you had, do you realize what exercising it would mean in practice? War. To put your demands into action, you'd have to conquer Russia by military force. That's your intention, is it?

Phob You know I don't mean that. You can't take me for a maniacal warmonger. I'm as far away as anyone could possibly be from the idea of an anti-Russian crusade. All I'm concerned about is the principle. And my principle implies the exact opposite of what you're ascribing to me. My central idea is that one should *keep one's distance*. If there's anything I'm trying to convince you of, it's solely that you should look upon the changes taking place in Russia *dispassionately* – you shouldn't get too involved in them. Of course there's no need to hinder them, but above all there's absolutely no need to *help* them! Don't welcome them with open arms! It's still far too early for that. If they really do want to change – and if they're really capable of it – they've got to do it on their own. If, as you're suggesting, the West should play an educative role towards Russia – if it should civilize them and put them back on the right track, it's got to be very strict and demanding with them. That's why all these promises to mend their ways, and these wishes to be taken into the European home should be met with a rather cool reception on our part. Not with a *refusal*, but just with a stern silence – that'll make them do some thinking. We've got to put their contrition to the test, to see if it's genuine. It's easy enough to make promises. In short, we should respond like this: 'So you want to live under one roof with us? Well, that's not entirely out of the question – but why not do a bit of work on yourselves for now, and let's see what comes of it?'

Phil You're determined to put them down. You just want to gorge yourself on the sight of their collapse. That's a mean and inhuman attitude, it's beneath the dignity of the true spirit of Europe. While calling for the protection of European values you're recommending means which are

basically at odds with them. The foundation stone of Western Europe is
its open-mindedness, its capacity to keep on absorbing and adopting new
elements. You can't save Europe by closing the door in Russia's face. If
we were to turn our backs on them right now, we'd be breeding a wolf in
our own backyard. Do you think if we spurn them they'll just weaken and
grow submissive, until they finally crawl up to us on their knees and beg
for mercy? Don't make me laugh! Humiliation and destitution certainly
won't make repentant sinners of them – on the contrary, they'll be driven
to a state of total barbarism. Remember Germany's humiliation after the
First World War, and the distinctly anti-German mood that pervaded
Europe then – that's what provoked them to retaliate, it paved the way
for Hitler. And Russia's far more touchy than Germany. It's even got an
obsession with being spurned, it's obsessed with the idea that the rest of the
world despises it. Personally, I think its military strength and superpower
status derive from this very obsession. 'If they're going to despise us,' the
Russians seem to think, 'if they're going to turn their backs on us, in
mockery or disgust, then let them at least be afraid of us. There's a price
to be paid for humiliating us.' The only result of locking them out in the
cold would be a big explosion. And history has known only two possible
outcomes of such a situation: either we'll conquer them and civilize them,
or else they'll conquer us. I reject the first possibility – for one thing, no
Westerner's ever yet managed to conquer Russia, neither Napoleon, nor
Hitler; so we're left with the second: suppose they conquer us. And that
isn't out of the question. Our youth is past and gone. We're old. But that
mustn't happen. Our Europe must *not* be *allowed* to die. It can survive,
but under one condition however: that it does not remain passive towards
the element of barbarity surrounding it. It must absorb that barbarity
into itself, and by so doing neutralize its ruinous effect. You claim that not
only is there nothing to be learned from them but even worse. We could
catch some sort of nasty illness from them. And that's where I utterly
disagree. I think all their years of living in poverty, under a threat, and
with a constant struggle, paradoxically enough, have given them something
valuable, which we ourselves are lacking. In order to survive, we must
strengthen our resistance, and we can only do that by taking ever larger
doses of poison. Homoeopathy – that's our only chance! In order to avoid
getting totally infected, you've got to get a little bit infected. In order to
be free of it, you've got to overcome it, and that means *partly taking it upon
yourself*. All the more since we're partly responsible: we didn't smother
communism at birth, although we could have done, and then we put up
with it for years, for at the end of the day *we were quite comfortable with it*;
the tyrannies gathering strength over there actually helped us keep stable,
by most efficiently scaring people away from Marxist pipe-dreams. And

now we have to pay for it. No no, not for the sake of decency, but out of common sense! The old Europe will save itself only if it can manage to dilute its blue blood by mixing it with the red blood of its plebeian cousins from the East. There's nothing to be afraid of, I tell you! We can't afford to be afraid!

Voice (*offstage through a megaphone*) Attention please! Attention please! Severe public disorder has broken out in the west end. Crowds of demonstrators are rioting and heading this way. The public are advised that it would be dangerous to remain in the park. I repeat, you remain in the park at your own risk. Attention, attention, you are advised to leave the park immediately by the *east* gate. Do not head for the west gate. I repeat: please leave the park by the *east* gate. Do not head for the west gate. Attention, attention . . . (*Fading but continuing.*)

Phil My God! Another riot! When'll there be an end to it? (*To* **Phob.**) Let's get out of here!

Phob Calm down! Why don't you finish what you were saying? (*Ambiguously, perhaps in all sincerity, perhaps feigning it.*) What you were just saying was very interesting. Just carry on a bit, and who knows, you might even convince me. That's what you wanted, isn't it?

Phil Are you out of your mind? How can we go on talking at a moment like this? Do you want to get your head kicked in?!

Phob What are you afraid of? They're not demonstrating against you, are they? And anyway, to judge from your opinions, you ought to be a supporter of theirs.

Phil However valid their demands, that form of protest is quite out of the question as far as I'm concerned.

Phob Hmm . . . I see.

Phil So, aren't you coming?

Phob I'm old, they won't do me any harm.

Phil As you like.

He runs off stage right.

Phob That's the *west* gate you're heading for.

Phil (*stopping in his tracks*) Oh my God, so it is! Thanks!

He runs off stage left.

Phob *gives a knowing smile.*

How Now Green Cow

Julie Burchill

How Now Green Cow was first performed at the Royal Court on 7 June 1990 with the following cast:

Woman   Sharon Bower

Girl   Lesley Manville

Directed by Max Stafford-Clark

The scene is set in a café/bar/brasserie – a tapas bar might be best. Two females of about thirty sit at a table. I want to suggest by their body language that they are friends of some long standing, yet not at ease with each other – possibly meeting after a row, or a long separation. There is much fiddling with ashtrays, accessories, crystals and coasters. The jumpiest one is a thin, pale, dark-haired, heavily made up girl in a tight black dress and black high heels, on the model of Louise Brooks, preferably with the perfect bob. She is chain-smoking. The calmer one is a heavyweight blonde wearing little make up, a subtle ski suntan and over-priced, over comfortable white jogging clothes and running shoes. She is obviously a woman; the brunette is still a girl. This, one should feel immediately, is at the heart of their antagonism.

Girl Are you drinking to remember, or drinking to forget?

Woman I'm not drinking at all, actually. (*Calls offstage.*) Just an *Aqua Libre* for me, please.

Girl Right. Got you. Well. I guess that means I'm drinking for two. (*Calls offstage.*) Two dry vodka martinis, garçon. Straight up. And when I say dry, I mean *bone.* Just let the vermouth *flash* at the vodka, then bang it up in the clink and throw away the key. Cheers. (*Looks combatively at other.*) So. How's life on the farm?

Woman (*warmly*) Wonderful. I can't *imagine* how I hacked it here for so long.

Girl Oh. Good. (*Sips drink.*) Don't you find it a little . . . *green*?

Woman (*enthusiastically*) Absolutely. That's what I love about it. No car alarms blaring, no Yuppies braying . . . and no having to have eyes in the bottom of your Timberlands. (*Leans across table.*) That's what finally drove us out. The *dogs.* The *fouling.*

Girl Right. Got you. (*Lights cigarette.*) Oh. You don't mind, do you?

Woman If you feel the need to poison your one and only body, go right ahead.

Girl Thanks. (*Shakes out match.*) Right. *Dogs.* I do know what you mean.

But between you and me, if you notice the dog do, your eyes are in the gutter, not on the stars. And when you quit having stars in your eyes, I guess it's time to go back where you came from. Where the supermarket closes at six and everyone knows your name. Though wanting to live in a place where everyone *does* know your name is just the consolation prize we go for when we realize we're also-rans in the race to make the *world* know our name.

Woman (*laughs*) Well, I think I'll settle for community spirit and clean streets, thanks!

Girl Really? How you've changed! When we were pubescent prisoners of the provinces, did we sit sobbing in our rooms, 'Oh, if only I could run away to London – *it's really clean there, with a great community spirit!*' Did we hell. We came here to *escape* cleanliness and community, not to find them. (*Drinks.*) Of course, we were young and brave then.

Woman You know, age is a very Western concept. In Africa, you'll find women don't think about ageing – they think about *growing*. And that's just the way I feel – that I'm growing.

Girl Yes – I thought you'd put on a few kilos.

Woman That's not what I mean and you know it. Listen, I'm sorry to be so judgemental so soon. But you've really got to get clear of this brat routine you've been running for the last twenty years. Growing up isn't anything to be scared of – it's a *gaining* process.

Girl (*Drinks.*) So you don't come up much any more, is that right?

Woman As little as I can. Which isn't much, thank God. I've got this wonderful machine – it does everything but throw the runes. I can send a design to Tokyo and get feedback within ten minutes – but it takes me a day to drive into London and home again with the same drawing. I come up once a fortnight, at most. And then it takes me three days to recover. London is so *ugly* – it's not even a focussed, energizing city like New York. The *hideous* new buildings, and the way they're *mutilating* the skyline –

Girl Not *that* one again. Tell me, what skyline is synonymous with man-made beauty? The Manhattan skyline. For a century we've oohed and ahhed at it from near and far. But let a few tallish buildings go up *here* – oh, soulless concrete jungle!

Woman That's different. We're *Europeans*.

Girl So? Of course your Paris and Venice are *prettier* than this old whore. But is it a city's business to be pretty? Isn't that what the countryside's there for? Because let me tell you, as if you didn't know; at the heart of every city lies some seriously unpretty things.

Woman Don't I know it! Greed, graft, envy, avarice, corruption . . .

Girl Love it to death! *That's* why the city was born. And to dress it up pretty – why, it's as morally duplicitous and metzobrow as putting a quilted cover on a toilet roll. We *all* know what's underneath. London is *meant* to be a monster. It's not Milton Keynes. It's a glittering neon catwalk that you look down on from your skyscraper late at night, tight on highballs, and you clench your fists and hiss like Tony Curtis in *The Sweet Smell Of Success*, 'God, I love this dirty rotten town!' That's the beauty of being in the belly of the beast, don't you see?

Woman (*stiffly*) Thank you for your dissertation. And done without notes, too. You should try it out at Speaker's Corner.

Girl Sorry. I was ranting. Was I awful?

Woman Very slightly.

Girl Sorry. It just gets on my wick when people put her down.

Woman Her?

Girl London. Everybody's doing it. And what they're carping about isn't really her at all. It's their own failure. They came to conquer the old trout, but she wasn't the walkover they imagined. London is the only city men talk about with the venom they reserve for ex-wives. (*Drinks.*) But you're right. I'm ranting. I must cool out.

Woman You know, that stuff isn't helping. It may *feel* as though it's part of the solution. But it's really part of the problem. You're just topping up the poison in your system – I can see the toxins shooting out of you in sparks.

Girl Like a cheapo carpet, you mean? (*Drinks.*) Mmm, that's *good*. If God passed water, it would taste like a dry martini.

Woman Why do you drink so much?

Girl Do I? Waiter, another please.

Woman You're drink dependent.

Girl Are you telling me I am an (*American accent.*) *alcoholic*? Goody. Does that mean I get to marry a President?

Woman It's not funny.

Girl It is, actually. The extent to which life's simple pleasures have been pathologized is very funny indeed. Not to mention tragic. Do you know that Mary Tyler Moore sought treatment for alcoholism because she found herself taking *two* martinis after a hard day's work? Two, after a long day having Dick Van Dyke's tongue down your throat. It's a dirty job but someone's got to do it. Now until very recently, taking two martinis after work was not called alcoholism, but *fun*. Which these days seems to be the vice that dare not speak its name. (*Slyly.*) Oh. What do alcoholic Buddhists chant?

Woman (*wearily*) I don't know. What *do* alcoholic Buddhists chant?

Girl Nam renge kyohoho and a bottle of rum! (*Falls about and splutters her drink.*)

Woman (*patiently*) Very droll.

Girl (*moodily*) Gee, thanks. (*Slyly.*) When's the wedding?

Woman Excuse me?

Girl The white. You look as though you had a bunk-up in a laundry van.

Woman When's the funeral, come to that?

Girl Oh my, I'm crushed! Honest, I really am. I've never heard *that* one before – that one and 'Cheer up, it might never happen!' (*Slyly.*) So where's the baby, then?

Woman (*suspiciously*) The what?

Girl The designer baby! Did you check it at the door with the rest of this season's accessories? Smart move. I bet that gear wouldn't look half so pristine after Rainbow finished chucking up her organic muesli on it.

Woman Her name, as you well know, is Saffron.

Girl Which sounds like a good excuse for matricide. 'She *made* me do it, Your Honour! – *she called me Saffron!*' 'Case dismissed, my child, and take a tenner from the poor box as you leave. You acted in the public interest.' (*Looks under table.*) And you're wearing running shoes! But you didn't run here, of course. Isn't that a bit like wearing a swimming hat to go shopping?

Woman (*irritably*) Why do you expect every woman under the age of seventy to deck herself out in a slit skirt and stilettoes every day of her life, even to walk the dog. I really think you ought to consider changing your style. You know, that whole power-dressing thing is *so passé*. And so *negative*. Why *should* a woman have to look like a man in order to be taken seriously?

Girl The opposite of power-dressing is power*less*-dressing; walk a mile in *those* shoes. And really, if the men *you* hang out with habitually get themselves up in slit skirts and stilettoes . . . well, I can understand at long last why you jumped the broomstick with Jeremy . . .

Woman Jonathan.

Girl But of course. (*Pause.*) Does *he* like you in running shoes?

Woman Yes.

Girl Bollocks. All men love high heels, black dresses and blowjobs. Even social workers. Even Masai tribesmen. Even *vegans*.

Woman That really is sexist garbage. And besides, I dress for *comfort*, not approval. But yes, Jonathan *does* like the way I look, he's not one of those Neanderthals who believe that a woman has to look like a drag queen to be attractive.

Girl There's always one who has to spoil it for everyone else. Is he minding Susan?

Woman *Saffron.*

Girl Listen, you may as well get used to calling her Susan. Because the minute she hits puberty, that's what she'll be calling herself. Remember Zowie Bowie? He's known as Joe these days. Moon Unit Zappa? Mike to you.

Woman Jonathan is *at home* with Saffron, yes.

Girl A real New Man, eh?

Woman If you *must* resort to sloppy journalistic clichés.

Girl I never met a sloppy journalistic cliché I didn't like. But listen, I'm not knocking him. At least he's going to get wise to the fact that motherhood's the only life sentence you get without committing a crime.

Not like the pantywaists who designed your lovely leisurewear. Or the rag
trade fag hags who compose hymns of praise to it. None of *them* will ever
be sitting at home like a lemon monitoring some screaming little vampire
in a Viyella vest. If *they* drop a puppy, they'll farm it out to some wretch
with a non-designer mouth to feed. Or worse still, they'll become Born
Again Cows and write pornographic books about giving birth in a vat of
lentils. And then they'll breastfeed it in public (and *only* in public, I can't
help but feel) until it can open beer cans with its teeth. And have you *seen*
those broads? It's always the ones with the lousy tits who feel the need to
whip them out everywhere. The punctured barrage balloon brigade. You
never see a nice bit of prime Lusardi B-cup on parade, have you noticed?
(*Wriggles lewdly.*) If you did, I'm sure I wouldn't object at all . . .

Woman You know, this may come as a shock to you. But the breast was
designed to feed babies. It's not something they're doing to offend you. Like
mooning.

Girl An inspired comparison. The anus was designed to defecate, and to
find like-minded souls who would attend all night showings of Bette Davis
films. But would you pull it out in public and put it through its paces?
Answer honestly now.

Woman That's a crude and obscene comparison and you know it. And
it's not even *funny*.

Girl You're right. I'm sorry – Bette Davis all-nighters are definitely no
laughing matter. Listen – I'll stop being personal, really I will. I'm just
trying to get a handle on you – you've really *changed*. It's like *Invasion of
the Bodysnatchers* – you've been *snatched*.

Woman (*gently*) No I haven't. I've just grown up.

Girl Well, maybe it's the same thing. (*Pause.*) You're a . . . a *Green*, aren't
you. (*Not a question; a statement.*)

Woman If you must slap a label on me. I would prefer to describe
myself as ecologically conscious. *Globally sentient*.

Girl I don't see you looking for some long-winded alternative when you
can write someone off as a Yuppie or a Sloane. But so; you're a Green,
and you work in the rag trade.

Woman No one has used that phrase since 1966.

Girl *Fashion*. OK? Now, how can *fashion* – which is by definition obsolescent – co-exist with conservation?

Woman You're not even *trying* to understand. Fashion *cares*. This year, we showed some really positive, life-affirming, *caring* fabrics; cashmere, linen, silk . . .

Girl All white now, natch. But what about the chemicals it took to get that white just right? And what about all the water, electricity and detergent it's going to take to keep it that way? And pardon my cheek, but how the frig can cashmere be described as 'caring'? What's so caring about spending a thousand smackers on a *poncho*? I'll tell you this for nothing – if those rag fags really cared, they'd clothe their flock in the cheapest, nastiest synthetic fibres they could find, and give the difference (and *what* a difference it is!) to the poor. Comprendez?

Woman Just because one is globally sentient does *not* mean one can't enjoy being a woman.

Girl It's a sad state of affairs when a woman defines herself by putting *on* clothes rather than taking them off. But what do I know? I'm *not* a woman, as you people seem determined that every human female past puberty must be. *Woman*; it's such an ugly, *defeated* word – womb-bound, earth-bound – some stolid, solid, short-legged, short-lived Lawrentian drudge, suffering in silence (and Salford). No thanks – I'll be a girl any day. Because girls are *bad*, and women are *good*; and goodness, as we should all know by now, is the booby prize men palm us off with to keep us down.

Woman But you're splitting hairs here. You can't deny that women – *females*, if you must – are *different*. Nurturing, giving, civilizing; our *values* are different.

Girl They're different because men moulded them that way. Man made woman like he made the noble savage; to carry the spiritual baggage that might weigh him down on the way to the top. Men have always liked morality in the way they like tennis; once a year, and strictly as a spectator sport. And the New Men are the worst.

Woman (*tolerantly*) Are you on drugs?

Girl I've heard them. Sitting in the juice bars. Lying in their teeth.'*Oh, I Really, Really admire women!* – *I wish I was one!* They're so *centred*, so *empowered* by the *Really, Really important* things in life! Wouldn't it be *awful* if they became like us.' *That's* the New Man-ifesto. And you know

what they call it where I come from? *Moving the goalposts*. If you don't
think we should put our names down for the rat race you shouldn't have
made it so much fun. Tell me – does Jonathan seriously believe that
women were happy *before* they came into contact with these dreadful male
ideas about ambition and success? Does he, perish the thought, think
housewives were *happy*? Now where have I heard that before? From men,
yes – but not New Men. Maybe there's no difference under the designer
stubble.

Woman Have you quite finished?

Girl Almost. You know, the funny thing is that the market's going to
prove a better friend than Marx ever did. It's ironic, don't you think, that
a shortage in the work force gets capitalism doling out crèches left right
and centre in a way that socialism couldn't manage in fifty years. There's
a moral there somewhere, and you can bake it in a fortune cookie and
serve it to Jonathan; 'Socialism says "Jam tomorrow, sister – so long as
you pick the fruit and stand by your man; just like that nice Mrs
Kinnock."'

Woman You've got to tell me something, and you've got to tell me the
truth. (*Leans across table.*) Did you vote for . . . Her, last time?

Girl I most certainly did and I'm proud of it. To become a radical Tory
is the most rebellious act a woman can perform. It scotches once and for
all all those smug, sexist theories about our essential *niceness*. Tell you
what, if any Green cow tells me again that just because I'm female I'm
also automatically caring and sharing, I'm going to kick her in the clit
and run. Just to show her the error of her ways.

Woman (*aghast*) I do not *believe* this. I'm hearing it and *I do not believe
this*. You are talking like a *fascist*.

Girl No, I'm talking like a *modern* – a rigorous mode of thinking we seem
to have abandoned recently in favour of Patience Strong homilies on
motherhood and Nature. And may I ask – what's in it for *us*? I can
understand what a *man* sees in Green – what better way to keep the little
woman barefoot and pregnant? After we get shot of all those nasty
energy-squandering time-saving devices, we'll be too busy cooking and
cleaning to get any uppity ideas about careers, Open University course or
extra-curricular cock. When it comes to a woman's place, Green is the
white man's Islam. (*Silence.*) Well, babes, you go ahead and be a woman.
But I personally will continue to enjoy being a girl. Which consists largely
of filling myself up with life-denying hormones, fast drugs, and a brace of

young black men who see me only as a body.

Woman (*aghast again*) Oh no. You're not *still* going that route, are you? It's so *dangerous* now. And besides, it's so *Seventies* – that *using* sort of sex.

Girl Sex without using is like eating without chewing – can't be done. You may live longer, but I'll die with a smile on my face.

Woman So that's the be all and end all of Madam's personal philosophy, is it? – drink, drugs and dick. Everything as a quick, consumable unit; no commitment and no consequences. You don't want a man – you want a *McDonalds*.

Girl Mmm – double relish.

Woman But where does that leave love? Where does love come into this self-satisfied little scenario?

Girl Right between my legs, that's where.

Woman You're talking about sex – which you can get on any street corner. I'm talking about love – which comes once in a lifetime. If you're lucky.

Girl But not for me, sweetheart. For me, love is a sexually transmitted disease – not the hot tub it is for you and Jonathan. You want to *tame* love, pull out its teeth – tame the beast, like one of those tranquilized lions lying around in the zoo. That's not my speed.

Woman Listen, I was too judgemental. I can see you're going through bad things right now. That you're not being properly nourished by your relationships. But you've got to try to get clear of it – and of the sort of men who confirm you lack of self-love. I'm not gloating here; but if you had the sort of quality relationship I have with Jonathan, you wouldn't talk this way. You just aren't meeting the right sort of man.

Girl Well its hard in public urinals – this wouldn't be our old friend *New Man* who's going to change my miserable little life, now would it?

Woman If you mean a man who's not afraid to show his vulnerability – then yes.

Girl Vulnerability is the new violence. They used to use their fists to get what they wanted – now it's their tear ducts. It's a great routine, for sure – but what it adds up to is blackmail minus the black eyes. *Look, you bitch – you made me cry!*

Woman Then what's *your* idea of a man?

Girl The usual. A mind that's weak and a body that's strong; a big schlong and a small brain. Just the opposite of New Man, I'm afraid. But then, those cocktail sausages tend to be impotent anyway, don't they? Which is just as it should be. I can never understand why people get so upset about impotence, myself – it's just your friend Mother Nature's way of telling a man he's a lousy screw.

Woman I can't *believe* what I'm hearing. Men are not just *phalluses*. They have feelings, just like us. And everyone knows now that size isn't important.

Girl The only women who think size isn't important are women who don't like sex. The smaller, the better; all the better to pretend it isn't *happening*.

Woman Listen, I know we haven't seen each other in a long time. But I had no idea that you'd been asleep for the past 40 years. Your sexual attitudes are straight out of a 1950s locker room.

Girl Which sounds like just the place I'd find my dream man. His idea of putting me on a pedestal would be sticking two pillows under my ass. Packing a foot and it ain't got toenails. Hung like a horse, goes all night and turns into a Lolita Lempicka frock in the morning. And *strong* – can carry my weekly shop on his dick, no hands. Because I'll tell you what; the suffragettes didn't throw themselves under racehorses so Baby here would have to take out her own garbage. That's what they're *built* for, the great hulking things – slave labour. And that's why New Man is such a grotesque mutation; he'd carry your child, if he could, but he won't carry your shopping! Really, who *needs* it?

Woman (*sips soft drink, controls temper, plays for time*) You know, I'm not mad at you. I'm just sad *for* you. You've got so much to give – so much love. But you're so into *competing* with men that you just can't focus on your strength as a *woman*. It's not just you – it's a neurosis that touches all of us Western women. I was in Africa last year – in Kenya – and the women there were amazing – so *strong*. In Latin America and the Middle East it's the same. But here, we've lost it. That confidence. That ability to go with the flow of the rhythm of the earth, and not live from one neurotic, artificial deadline to another. That *strength*.

Girl (*pause. Incredulously*) Excuse me – but would these be the same African women who are still having their clitori sliced off en masse, the way rural retards cut the tails off terriers?

Woman Will you just –

Girl Would these be the same Middle Eastern women who are stoned to death for adultery and executed for being raped? Pardon my confusion, but are you suggesting that I take these women as *role models*?

Woman There. You see? It's pointless even *trying* with you. You just *refuse* to even attempt to understand the culture and traditions of people anywhere outside your own totally ethnocentric line of vision. It's hopeless. I don't know why I bothered.

Girl You know what tradition is? It's a fancy way of saying 'This is what we've done round these parts for a long time now. We don't know why we started, but we're too scared to change.' And if *we'd* stuck to *our* traditions, we'd be running around in woad, witch-burning and bear-baiting. You people – your logic is *shot*. It's OK to murder and mutilate women in the name of superstition, but it's not OK to cut down trees in the name of survival! Where do you *get* these ideas? – where's the *rest* of you! Because you seem to have a little piece of something missing. You seem to feel the rape of the countryside (as you insist on calling it) but not the rape of Arab women. You can hear the cries of Latin American trees being cut down – but not the cries of Latin American people. Let's face it; Green is politics for people who don't like people. For people who've been turned on once too often by those they tried to help. The great thing about whales, see, is that they're not going to spit in your face and call you Whitey. I mean, I'm sure it feels great from where you're sitting. On those nights when Jeremy can't get it up, it must be nice to roll over and know the rainforest loves you anyway. But please don't confuse this cosmic afterglow with anything serious like changing the world. Because you're going to be in for one big post-coital triste.

Woman (*hissing*) Listen, you're out of line, you! I've been putting up with your negativity, and that big red running sore in the middle of your face that you call a mouth all night! And now *I've* got something to say to *you*.

Girl Listen, if it's about my negativity, don't bother. I'm so negative, every time I put chemicals up my nose, photographs pop out of my ears.

Woman (*patiently*) It's my own fault. I indulged you. As people always do with you. But I'm through as of now. How *dare* you sit there and tell me I am not a people person!

Girl Well, you –

Woman (*resorting to old tough vernacular*) Button the lip for one minute, can't you? Seeing you again has made me angry, but it's also made me sad. It's not just me who's changed. It's *you*. The girl I used to know. The bad girl with the big crazy heart. She's gone.

Girl God, *no*. Are you by any chance trying to tell me I've 'sold out'? Cliché city! Where do you think we are – the National Theatre!

Woman I've had to listen to you ranting about everything from sex to skylines tonight. But what it's all boiled down to is one note – ME–ME–ME–ME–ME! Because everything – people, politics, the planet – just exists for you to suck, fuck and chuck. You don't give a damn whether the Earth dies, just so long as you die with a smile on your face. And that's the great dream of our so-called culture; that everyone can have everything forever and ever, world without end. That we can all go at the world's resources like one of those crazy American housewives running round a hypermarket with ten minutes to fill up the cart. That we can go at the world like pigs at a trough. Smorgasbord. And now we're selling it to the rest of the world. Only what happens when 500 billion people decide they want everything for ever? I'll tell you. There will be 500 billion dead people lying across the aisles. Drowning in the trough. And they won't have smiles on their faces, or be good-looking corpses like Madam. They'll have cancer of the skin because we destroyed the ozone layer; poison in their lungs because we polluted the air. Swollen, starved bodies because we turned the forests into deserts. And why are we doing this? Why are we committing mass suicide? Just so you can die with a smile on your face.

Girl But I –

Woman Christ! *You* again! I don't know if you're aware of this, but it is a scientific fact that the world revolves around the *sun*, not *you*. *You* like a good time – what about the billions of people not yet born? Don't they deserve one too? Don't they deserve a better birthright than a dying world?

Girl Of course.

Woman Then stop fighting us. We're on the same side, you and me.

We're custodians of this small, beautiful planet.

Girl OK. Oh, waiter, when you've got a minute – sick bag, please. Listen, I don't want a bunch of dead penguins on my conscience, no one does. The way you try to *blackmail* people – you're worse than the Catholic Church. Well, here's one pagan you're *not* going to convert. We may inhabit the same planet, but we live in different worlds. I'm not a child of the universe. I'm a creature of this monster century. Sure. I'll sign your petitions. But I won't give up my faith for yours. Because mine got me where I am today.

Woman If your life's so peachy, what are you so afraid of? Why do you feel the need to escape from life with enough drink and drugs to kill a small horse?

Girl A candyass like you can't even begin to understand that they take me *deeper* into life, not out of it. It's *you* that's on the run. *Country cottage. Aqua Libre!* All that crap about the city! – when people knock the city, they mean one thing. It isn't car alarms or garbage they hate – it's *people*. People *are* the city. But listen, I understand. If *I'd* put on the tonnage you have lately, I'd be seriously moist for seals too. For sure, none of them's ever going to turn round and call you Fatso.

Woman (*standing up*) You bitch! Jonathan was *right* about you! NO – I WON'T! (*Sits down and begins to massage back of neck, while doing Buddhist chanting.*)

Girl (*mortified*) Oh my God. Everyone's looking! (*Hissing.*) Quit that!

Woman (*smiling serenely*) There. That's better. (*Gathers together effects.*) I want to apologize for my bad reaction there. It was intolerable. There's no excuse. Even if you did provoke me. And I'm sorry, but I really don't think either of us is being nourished by this interface. Shall we call it a draw, and call it a day?

Girl (*moodily*) Call it what you like. Like you call clitorectomy culture. It's still called backing off where I come from.

Woman (*momentarily becoming a girl again*) I have never backed off in my *life*, you bitch, and you know it!

Girl That's more like it! That's more like *you*. Now, what was it got your goat there? You said I accused you of not being (*American accent.*) 'a people person'. Well, show me I'm wrong. Tell me the last time the rag trade threw a bash for incest survivors.

Woman I'm a bit hazy on that. I'll have to get back to you, but AIDS, for instance –

Girl Ah, AIDS – every rag hag's pet cause. But what shade of AIDS is flavour of the month, may I ask? Those wretched Rumanian babies? Those millions of dying Africans? Why, no – hush my mouth. You'd sneer at the sort of bigot who claimed that charity begins at home every time the Government sends a few bundles of used teabags to Ethiopia – but when it comes to AIDS, some pallid poofter gets your money every time. After all, what do we know of some black or some baby in some faraway land? Except that they wear *really* bad clothes, and *obviously* don't have any *style*. White men and trees – that's where the rag trade's heart is. Even though twice as many women die from cervical cancer each year as men do from AIDS. But how many of your fag designer friends are going to 'come out' for *women's trouble*?

Woman Look – I take your point. We'll have to get with the cervical cancer programme. I'll run it through the machine as soon as I get home. I'll organize a lunch next week to monitor feedback. But you've got to understand that the rainforest is *dying* . . .

Girl So are people. Don't cry for anything that can't cry for you –

Woman Last month we had a masked Venetian ball for the rainforest, and we –

Girl May I ask how much the tickets were?

Woman A thou a pair, I think.

Girl Might I be right in thinking this was a rather *exclusive* affair?

Woman We don't think in those outmoded, class-ridden terms.

Girl Of course we don't. We just prefer to be with our own kind. You don't see squirrels hanging out with pigs. And you don't see artists hanging out with artisans. Unless it's some divine little tribal chieftain with a bone through his nose.

Woman You don't know what you're talking about. We're just ordinary, hard-working, focussed people –

Girl The caste of characters at this masked ball, where the blind lead the blind? Pop stars. This year's models. A gaggle of aristos. A giggle of debs.

Minor Royalty, in a slow season. All frugging away in that half-assed way
rich people do – stiff in all the wrong places. And just a brace of peasants,
to add spice. It's interesting, this line up. So far as I can tell, this is the
first moral crusade led by the seriously rich. And why? BECAUSE THEY
OWN THE PLANET! Of *course* they want it to be in good nick when
they pass it onto the sprogs, with the family silver and the ancestral seat.
They're friends of the earth because it's been a damn good friend to them.
Can't you see how grotesque the green dreams of the rich look to the
poor? A sick joke – like Marie Antoinette playing milkmaids.

Woman You're *wrong*. The planet belongs to *all* of us. *Equally*. Ecology
recognizes no barriers – race, creed or colour. *Or* gender, come to that.
We'll all live or die together. Green means co-existing peacefully instead
of competing mindlessly. It means living in harmony, *side by side*; not on
top, not underneath. Just living peacefully *together* – like people *used* to.

Girl Excuse me. But are you telling me that before people started carrying
Filofaxes, they lived *happily* together? The history of the *world* before
capitalism was just one tribe after another wiping out anyone different
they could lay their hands on. And if no one different was around, they'd
do it to their own kind. Do you recall a certain self-motivated broad
called Boadaceia?

Woman Boudica.

Girl Whoever. But she certainly could throw a shoe. Listen, since
capitalism put its soothing hand on the world's fevered brow there's been
less conflict – people don't want to see their corporate investment go up in
smoke, is why. If I as a Yankee industrialist and bank-roller of the
Republican Party build a billion dollar plant in the Soviet U, am I going
to sit by and see it get its ass bombed? No. I'm going to get on the blower
to Bushy baby, and by the time I've hauled him through the
mechanically-recovered meat machine he's going to find a more *civilized* way
of settling his differences with Friend Mikhail. Believe me, there's no
deterrent like investment.

Woman If you went to Africa, or Brazil, you'd find that all your smart-
ass arguments just melted away in the face of the beauty and dignity of
the people. And you'd be lost for words. For once.

Girl If I went to Brazil or Africa, or Mars for that matter, I'd find one
thing – the confirmation of my long-held belief that everyone wants indoor
toilets and Madonna records. You like their craftwork so much, *you* do it
– I'm sure they'll throw in a date with Mother Nature, too. Yeah, they've

got her number. In Armenia, after the earthquake. In Ethiopia, after the
famine. She's outstayed her welcome in the Sudan a few times, I can tell
you. Whoa! Way to go mother N! Whomp them Armenians, starve them
Sudanese. What a baad mother you are – go and tell *them* how great she
is. Why, you're likely to get sent home in one of those attractive
wickerwork baskets you admire so much in your Oxfam catalogue. Asking
Mother Nature to look after you is like asking Myra Hindley to babysit.
But of course I know why you've got the hots for her. We all love to
watch wildlife films on TV – even me. The majestic wildebeest sweeping
across the Serengette; the gentle giant gorilla who has learned well the
ancient Buddhist wisdom that he who speaks does not know while he who
knows does not speak. Animals. Being *natural*. A jacuzzi for the soul.
Until that moment when the cheetah leaps on the lithe, life-affirming
gazelle – AND TEARS ITS THROAT OUT! YEUUUCH! 'Why did
they have to put that in?' – Sam Peckinpah has crashed the Garden of
Eden. Well, no one put that in. That's *Nature* for you. In the raw. She
isn't some fat, benign broad baking bread in a stripped pine kitchen. *She
isn't Sheila Kitzinger*. She's the biggest serial killer the world has ever seen.
And they'll never stop her now. Because she's got friends in high places.
She's got God on her side.

Woman Well, you can still talk up a storm – I'll give you that. But
that's all it is – *words*. Words in a sterile, air-conditioned vacuum. If you
actually took the time to go and see how people live – instead of putting
all your money up your nose – you wouldn't be able to sit there and write
off the rest of the world so slickly. Because people *do* live in harmony with
Nature – when our aerosols and exhaust pipes aren't turning their delicate
balancing act into some fight to the death if we leave them alone. And
they *can* teach us; no matter what crimes are committed on their bodies,
that wisdom never leaves them. Why, I bet they could even teach *you* how
to get back in touch with your natural wisdom. If you'd shut up for a
minute and let them.

Girl You know, I'm so sick of hearing about these faraway places with
strange-sounding names, wherein dwell these wise and just beings who live
life as she was lived before the Fall. And I'm sick in particular of being
told by the ruling family of this country that we white trash could *rilly,
rilly* learn something from these noble savages. Learn what, pray? Foot-
binding? Bride-burning? Make mine mixed-up Western alienation any day.
Yes, if I was the Clown Prince I think I'd be inclined to keep my head
down when it came to praising the rural life. Because if I remember
rightly, the ruling class of this country didn't have too much respect for

their natives when they forced us off our farms and into their factories.
From which the Family Windsor has reaped the benefits ever since.

Woman   There! You said it! Don't you *dare* take it back! You said that
life was better before industry!

Girl   Au contraire, Pierre. I said it was bad *logic* for our leaders to praise
a lifestyle they stopped us from living. But I didn't say it was a bad *move*.
The industrial revolution was probably the best thing ever to hit this
island, with the possible exception of Oscar Wilde and Lycra. The rural
idyll was never real; just a rough sketch for a theme park, created by city
dwellers. Nature was what we had before Laura Ashley; if Nature hadn't
existed, we would have had to create it. *And we did.* Because Nature
evolves, like everything else. *Being modern is now natural for us.* And to strip
it away would be as inhumane as stripping away the culture of those
Amazonian Indians you care so much about. You people hate theme
parks, right? But if we all went back to that rural idyll, back to *Nature*,
can't you see what a theme park that would be? And wouldn't the
Americans love it! 'Gee, quaint little England – it's so *Green!*' Green is the
colour of snot, money and ignorance. Which just about sums up your
movement. *Mooovement.* How now, Green cow.

Woman   (*gathering things together*)   Right. That's it. Your fifteen minutes are
up. This whole meet was a terrible mistake. A total waste of space and
interface. I've had it with you. Goodbye. (*Stands up.*)

Girl   (*reaching across table and grabbing wrist*)   Wait. Remember? When we
were young? What we wanted? The biggest birthright this century gave
girls like us was the chance to be born again, just by re-creating ourselves. Do
you remember how natural it felt to make yourself up from scratch? In the
long back bedroom summer holidays, hell, it was a lot more fun, and a lot
less like hard work, than it was for our uptight parents to do it in the first
place. Do you know, my parents never once had sex on their honeymoon?
Because they were too ashamed at the thought of getting gunk on sheets
someone else would have to wash. My mother told me that, one night
when the egg flip had been flowing. Christmas, I think. Woman's
confidence. Being ashamed – that's what being a woman means to me.
You come from the Capodimonte Culture too. That's our tradition. And
we escaped. So can you just explain to me why you want to turn your
back on everything we ever fought for? I'll try to understand, honest I
will. But can't you see how reactionary this all is? *To conserve – conservative.*
Whatever happened to pulling the sucker down and seeing where the pieces
fall?

Woman It doesn't work, baby. I've tried it. I've had three abortions and two breakdowns in twelve years – I can't go another round. I just want to get fat and old in peace. And if I have to pretend that everything's fine with Jeremy –

Girl Jonathan.

Woman AH, fuck it – he's a Jeremy, if ever there was one. If I have to live in the sticks and bake bread and rub crystals like some demented loon to buy the space I need to sort my life out, I'll do it. Maybe this Green thing does make me feel better about myself. But I need it. People need roots.

Girl (*banging fist on table*) THEY DON'T! Trees need roots – people need *courage*, and faith in the future. You *can't* go over to them, I won't *let* you; we swore we'd never go back? Well, you're going back by going Green – in return for a piddling little peace of mind. It's selling out of the worst kind – because it feels like opting in.

Woman It's easy for you. You're strong. You're beautiful. You're still young –

Girl I am six months and three days older than *you* – it's the healthy living that makes you feel old. And I'm not as strong as you think. I know what you're scared of because I'm scared too. This modern life is life without a safety net. And when it gives you tired thirtysomethings one sleepless night too many, and your perf at the office isn't hitting the max, what could be easier than to run home to Mother Nature? With her tits down your throat, you'll nod out in no time on the milk of instant amnesia. But listen, whatever gets you through the night. Hell, I do drugs too. So pig out. *Enjoy.* But what I want, just this once, just for me, is the truth; All About Green. Admit that it's nothing more than moral cowardice masquerading as social conscience. That it's the middle-aged spread of the grey matter, for people who need a philosophy to support their soft underbellies. It's the penitence of those who never had it so good as in the sleazy, easy, sexy, greedy Eighties, and can't handle the kicks without the kickback. I want you to admit that Green is the last refuge of those who are frightened of freedom. *Frightened of life.*

Woman (*looking up into* **Girl***'s face*) You want me to admit that? Throw away my last illusion?

Girl Yes.

Woman (*shaking free*) Never. I'll kill you first.

Girl (*laughing*) You wouldn't have the stomach for it. You're a herbivore now, remember? MOOOOO. MOOOOO.

Woman *pulls a small revolver from bag and points it at* **Girl**.

Girl MOOOOO. MOOOOO.

Woman Survival of the fittest, sweetie. That's what we believe in.

Shoots.

Girl collapses over table.

Pause.

Girl (*looking up, dazed*) God. You *cow. You bitch.* (*Sits up gingerly.*) What's in the piece?

Woman Big blanks. We used them at Sebastian's show. Variations on the Wild West End.

Girl You *bitch.*

Woman (*untying her running shoes, throwing them offstage. Seems like a girl now, not a woman*) God, I needed that. I feel ten years younger. And ten pounds lighter.

Girl We'll make a carnivore of you yet.

Woman Go slow, my gums are soft. (*Smiles seductively at* **Girl**.) Bang bang – you're born again. Only seven lives to go. So what are you drinking?

Girl Triple vodka martini. For my nerves.

Woman Waiter, two triple vodkatinis toot sweet. And while you're at it, line up the next round – I hate that wait between drinks. Yes – straight up; with a twist.

The Wall-Dog
(Der Mauerhund)

Manfred Karge

English version by Howard Brenton from a translation by Jane Brenton

The Wall-Dog was first performed at the Royal Court on 7 June 1990 with the following cast:

Hound	Jonathan Cullen
Guard	Gary Olsen

Directed by Nancy Diuguid

One

The Berlin Wall, with a gap in it. Sleeping by the wall, the Border **Guard**. *The* **Hound** *emerges from his concrete kennel, and wakes his master.*

Hound
Guard! Forgive
     The early morning call
But we've got a border crosser
     On the anti-Fascist security wall!

Guard
Get your great
     Soppy paw
Down off me –
     Year in, year out
I did my duty, now
     I don't care no more.

Hound
Don't get it, don't get it!
     All the border crossers
That I bit
     And then you shot?
Is that all forgiven and forgot?
     How can we turn round and be
A normal man with a normal dog?

Guard
Orders is order and the orders is
     Now we are at peace
Tell you what I think –
     Peace is piss
But that's the cup we have to drink
     So let me alone, go
Dig a bone . . .

The **Hound** *bangs his head against the wall.*

Guard
Hey wall-hound!
    Don't try to eat
The wall down
    The concrete'll break
Your teeth . . .

Hound
Under Marx we had the best
    Jolly ideology
Great days, all dissent
    Stamped out –
Medals for bravery upon your chest
    Karl gave us the power
To snarl and shout
    I did last year –
I remember the lovely taste
    Of human fear
When I sank my face
    Into five border crossers
In one day.
    So what are you trying to say
My hero of the Fatherland?
    Do you want to live
In America? Do you want
    The land of the free?
Have you gone soft on me?

Guard
Dog, get off my wick
    Not one kick
Have you ever had from me
    Crouched down by the wall
In all weathers, I'd
    Fill your bowl with water
Brush your coat and get
    A big beef bone for your tea.

Hound
Hang on! Where's your medal?
    Your order of socialist gallantry?

You've flogged it for hard currency
    To a tourist by the wall
The head of Karl Marx
    for a couple of Western Deutschmarks
The hammer and sickle
    For a dime and a nickel . . .

Guard
Not true!

Hound
You flogged it
    Didn't you!

Guard
That will do!

Hound
Was it just for lies and deceit
    All for nothing
That I cut my paws
    To bits on the people's concrete
Leaping at the throat
    Of a bastard agent
Of filthy capital
    Trying to climb the anti-fascist wall?
Howl howl!
    Listen – there's one of them
Out there now.

Guard
Why shouldn't a citizen
    Go for a night-time stroll?

Hound
Not by our wall!

Guard
Normal behaviour in a normal world.

Hound
Maybe he's got money
    Maybe he's rich
Once you thought differently

You'd have left the bastard
Dead by the wall in a ditch.

Guard
Can you smell
      The guy?
Can you tell
      What he's got on him?

Hound
I sniff a profiteer –
      From the West
Come over here
      To pick up what he can.
I could weep
      For the GDR
We are
      A prey for Western vices
A bargain basement
      With knockdown prices –
Don't fall asleep!

Guard
Why not?
      Next to a shot
Of Schnapps
      Sleep's the great
Bringer of oblivion –
      Hey, Fritz!
A hare – I'll shoot
      It for you!
You're on
      For a treat –
See, my love for my dog
      Is sacred and true.

Hound
Leave the animal
      I can't eat.

Guard
Eating is your Schnapps
      Your cup

Of oblivion – there
    Goes the little sod.
Right, he dies
    Your brother
Can gobble him up.
    No compromise!

The **Guard** *shoots and runs off.*

Two

The **Hound** *puts on a gas mask and peers through the hole in the wall. Then he turns away, fetches a small red book from the kennel, and reads.*

Hound
You slaves of money
    Crueller than your ruler

You bankers and landlords
    And vicious lackeys, bare

Your fangs, gorge your mouths
    With foaming blood and dance

Howling at the eye
    In Capital's night sky, your

Fantasy moon –
    The mighty eye

Blind with grief and loathing
    That dare not see

Over the fields, dare
    Not face the sight

Of nature and mankind
    Disfigured in the night.

Three

The **Guard** *returns with the dead hare. The* **Hound** *creeps away to his kennel.*
The **Guard** *waves his booty back and forth in front of the kennel opening.*

Guard
Lovely juicy bunny meat! (*Pause.*) Yum yum yum! (*Pause.*) Where's my
little one, then? (*Pause.*) Where's he gone, then? (*Pause.*) Heel, Fritz, Heel!
(*He lays the hare on the ground, bends over it, as though he wants to eat it.*)
Yummy yummy! No phoney hare, this, from the guardroom mess, oh no!
Yum yummy! (*He stands up again.*) Come on then, Fritzi, come on! (*Suddenly*
yells.) Dog! Get out here! (*Pause.*) Still won't. There. (*Throws the hare into*
the kennel. The **Hound** *throws it back again. The* **Guard** *flings it in a rage*
through the hole in the wall.) Guten appetit! (*He approaches the kennel again.*)
Don't make it harder for me than it already is, laddie.

Turns away, cries. The **Hound** *looks out of his kennel in sympathy and approaches*
the **Guard***.*

Hound
Don't cry, comrade, I don't mean
    To criticize. I remain serene
Serene as a killing machine
    Can be. Get the hare
I'll eat the lot
    Crack
That bunny's bones
    Skin, brain, gut, fur . . .

Guard
Great! I'll get it back
    For you.

The **Guard** *climbs through the hole in the wall to the other side. The* **Hound**
fetches plate and cutlery out of the kennel and ties a napkin under his chin. When
the **Guard** *returns with the hare, instead of his military cap he wears a felt*
hat.

Guard
Dear wall-dog
    Slob of a dog
Please, at your pleasure, gob
    Down this bit
Of canine high cuisine.

Hound
Guard – what's
    On your head?

Guard
What?

Hound
    That

Guard
That is my new hat.
    What else?

Hound
That's a capitalistic hat!
    That on your head
Will get you dead.

Guard
The hat goes
    With the new job.
New job
    New hat
And that is that.

Hound
Not clever,
    Guard,
Off with that hat
    Or you'll get bit.

Guard
Down down, corporal Fritz
    I'm pulling rank –
Sit!

The **Hound** *obeys.*

What hat to get your head beneath
    That is the question.

Hound
You mean wear the right hat
    And all the rest is shit
Your hat is where it's at?

Guard
Right, dog!
    This is a new situation.
Punishment, dog! Turn tragedy
    Into farce – recite
All military regulations
    Backward, tip to arse
And now. See that hare there?
    That hare
Is now a pair of trousers.

It happens. The **Guard** *puts on the trousers*

Magic man, that's me –
    Now all I need's
A camel hair coat
    Briefcase, brolly
And in a twinkling
    I am free.

Coat, bag and brolly appear.

Now, dog
    Let's hack it
With Capitalism's magic
    On you.
Your relatives – I mean
    The Rottweiler population
They are a profoundly
    commercial proposition
You can
    Travel the world
As a savage dog salesman
    Each cur
Guaranteed bred
    Straight out of you.
All you need is
    Some simple proof
That you are not now and have never been
    A red.

Hound
No magic
    No proof –

Better dead
    Than never having been
A red.

Guard
Let's try again –
    There is a big demand
For big dogs like you
    In South Korea –
I'm talking dogmeat here
    For a fast food chain –
Shake? Agreed?
    Now all we need to do
Is calculate
    The retail price
Of the meat on you.

Hound
Being a hamburger
    In South Korea?
That's not my idea
    Of a new career.

Guard
Then I'll flog your canine talents
    To a firm in Switzerland
They need lots of doggies
    For pharmacological experiments
In laboratories.

Hound
The Swiss
    Or South Korea
I've got a better idea –
    Resist!

Guard
Up against the wall
    Dog, you've kissed
The old life 'bye 'bye –
    The Swiss or South Korea
Heads or tails
    Call!

Hound
Is that my twist
    Of fate?

Guard
You've said it, pal –
    Come on I can't wait

Hound
Hell
    In Korea
Or hell in Switzerland?
    No thanks! I'm not the dog
That licks the oppressor's hand –
    I'll get into domestic politics
I'll form a pack
    Of comrade democratic dogs
That fights
    For the people's rights.

Guard
A werewolf in the red resistance?
    Face reality
You'll get no assistance
    In this country –
Haven't you noticed? Suddenly
    We are all good Prussians
Bourgeois Mecklenburgers
    And solid Saxons
Cringe, dog, come to heel
    Your left-wing actions
Have no appeal.

Hound
The Swiss or Korea –
    Right! I've got another idea
It makes my legs go limp.
    But I don't care.
I'll sell myself to a pimp.
    I'll be obscener
Than a hyena
    But better a whoremaster
Kicking my head

Than the pain
Of diodes stuck in my brain –
    Nor will I be killed and grilled
Dead in the greater cause
    Of the faster
Cheese burger

Guard
Dog, you're far too picky –
    Don't you see just how sticky
Your position is?
    Get your muzzle around this –
My service revolver
    Will be the sudden resolver
Of your shilly-shallying.

Hound
Switzerland or South Korea?
    I know!
I'll trade in fear
    I'll be a quisling
Turn turncoat,
    I'll inform on the old regime
On a professional basis –
    For cash I'll put the names
To faceless faces
    Why not? Others
Affect a sudden transformation
    And betray their brothers
Treachery is a great rewarder
    In our brand new German order –
Yesterday's party secretary
    And stern ideologue
Finds it as natural as
    The morning dew
To be a member of the CDU
    And, overnight, embrace the stress
Of scribbling for the tabloid press.
    So why shouldn't an old regime
Wall-dog
    Turn his wolf-coat inside out
And get his snout
    Into the cream?

Guard
Bravo
    Fritz, my friend –
But it's
    Too late, you will end
In Switzerland
    Or South Korea
You know it's true
    I'll have to shoot you
If you don't.

Hound
I'd count
    The petals of a flower
But I can't see one –
    I don't have the power
To talk of mercy
    For a savage dog that's just not done.

Guard
Too many moans and groans
    From you
Life's not all marrow bones
    And sausages and beer
Y'know –
    Switzerland and South Korea
Will grow on you.

Makes up his mind.

Look, I don't care, but
    this will cheer you up –
This will make you feel
    A real
Little pup again.
    Actually I am a woman.

He drops his trousers, revealing suspenders. Music is heard.

Hound

Song.

In the middle of the night
    In the tight moonlight
Whoever would have thought it

Whoever would have thought it
    That his lovely legs
Would shine so bright

Whoever would have thought it

Guard
In the middle of the night
    In the tight moonlight
Giving you a flash

Of my lovely legs
    And me selling you
For dollars, cash

You and me
    And me selling you
For dollars, cash

In the middle of the night
    In the tight moonlight
Whoever would have thought it

Hound
In the middle of the night
    Under a bitter moon
Money was your tune

Whoever would have thought it
    You rattled my bones
And I threw stones

At you from off the wall
    You showed your lovely legs
For a flash of cash that's all

In the bright moonlight
    Under the hangdog moon
In the middle of the night

Whoever would have thought it

The **Hound** *breaks a piece of stone from off the wall.*

Guard
In the middle of the night

Whoever would have thought it
A dog threw a stone

Signed his own
    Death warrant
In the bright moonlight

His life was a stone thrown
    In the bright moonlight
In the middle of the night

Whoever would have thought it.

The **Hound** *has raised the stone against his master. The latter shoots it down with his pistol.*

Guard
OK my friend
    That stone
Was the end for you
    Now all I've got to do
Is draw up a bill of sale
    For the parts of one male
Dog.

The **Guard** *writes on the wall in chalk the accounts for the sale of the* **Hound**. *The latter takes off his head and steps forward.*

Guard
Liver seventy
    Twenty for each lung
Sixty nine for the tongue
    The balls for fifty
A special offer
    Ten marks off
For all the offal
    Bone marrow, spleen
Fifteen
    Ear-wax? Three fifty
Thirty the ears, nose, chin
    Ninety for the heart
Every part
    A bargain,
Now minus seven plus three
    To calculate The VAT

Hound
So in the dark
    Of the new order
My master sends me to the butcher's knife
    Toting up the profit of the slaughter
Of his faithful wall-dog's life –
    I won't protest, not a snarl
Not a whimper not a bark.

Guard
One hundred and forty eight –

Hound
Now a bow wow not a miaow –

Guard
And for a back leg
    Ninety –

Hound
I'll not resist
    Not a howl
At the moon
    Not a wail
Of canine pain
    Not a clenched fist
In the communist salute
    Certainly not a Siegheil
I'll leave
    The fighting and the biting
Up to others now.

Guard
The bile and the juice
    of a dog's belly
Reserved specially
    For a rare Asian soup –
That'll produce
    Another fifty.

Hound
It's all the same to me
    This savage hound
Rests his head upon his paw

His muzzle on the ground
Dumb, a dumb wall-dog.
I'll say no more.

The **Hound** *keeps his mouth tight shut, while the* **Guard** *with increasingly violent movements does his sums upon the wall. Music starts up and slowly drowns out the figures snapped out by the* **Guard**. *As it gets darker, a last faint ray of lights falls on the silent* **Hound**.

Disneyland It Ain't

Sue Townsend

Disneyland It Ain't was first performed at the Royal Court Theatre Upstairs on 18 June 1990 with Carole Hayman as Maureen.

Characters:

Maureen

Mr Mouse

Directed by Richard Wilson

Sound of fairground jollity. Kids screaming. Lights up to show **Mr Mouse**. *He is wearing Mickey Mouse boxer shorts and braces. He sits smoking. He slumps forward. He is tired. He is also in pain, he holds his ear. He winces.*

Maureen, *an Englishwoman enters. She is upper working-class. Mid-forties. Her pastel casual clothes have been bought especially for the trip to Florida. She is a shy woman, who has nursed a dying child for two years. She sees* **Mr Mouse** *and starts back. She watches as* **Mr Mouse** *stubs out his cigarette. When he stands, she approaches him.*

Mo Excuse me Mr Mouse. (**Mr Mouse** *swings round.*) Your colleague Mrs Mouse said you'd be here. I wonder if I could have a word?

Mr Mouse *points to his watch, then waves and starts to leave.*

Mo I will be quick. I'm a woman who has very little time. The thing is Mr Mouse, my daughter is dying in a hotel room, will you come to the hotel and give her your blessing?

Mickey I ain't a priest. I ain't even religious. And you ain't supposed to see me in my underwear. It's a priest you want, you'll find one in the book.

Mo She's not religious either, she's only ten. It's you she wants to see.

Mr Mouse I don't know no dying kids.

Mo She knows you, she's known you since she first opened her eyes. She had your wallpaper on the wall next to her cot. We didn't use it on every wall. Her seventh word was mouse. Will you come to the hotel?

Mr Mouse Why should I?

Mo Because it would make her happy.

Mr Mouse I ain't got time.

Mo Your shift finished ten minutes ago.

Mr Mouse Who told you?

Mo Mrs Mouse.

Mr Mouse Bitch! I got this thing to do.

Mo I'll pay you.

Mr Mouse How much?

Mo Fifty dollars.

Mr Mouse Ain't worth starting my car for that.

Mo How much do you want?

Mr Mouse I don't want nothin', I gotta go.

Mo One hundred dollars?

Mr Mouse How do you know she's dying?

Mo I'm an expert on the subject of dying children.

Mr Mouse You seem just like a regular woman to me, you ain't a doctor that's for certain.

Mo I've spent two years watching children die. I've seen their hair fall out, I've seen their eyes get bigger in their heads, I've seen them in such pain . . . I know there's not a God. He would never allow it.

Mr Mouse That's a bad thing to say, I ain't religious but I sure as hell *know* there's a God.

Mo You can't *know*.

Mr Mouse Listen, I had plenty of people *tell* me there's a God. People with *diplomas*.

Mo But you're not religious?

Mr Mouse I ain't been to church since I was a kid. You're British ain't you?

Mo English.

Mr Mouse Same thing ain't it?

Mo No, I am not Scots, or Welsh or Irish, any more than you're Canadian or Mexican.

Mr Mouse You a visitor to Disneyland?

Mo No, to you. We came to see you.

Mr Mouse Not *me*, Thomas Harton Wilberforce?

Mo We came to see Mr Mouse.

Mr Mouse They ain't the same thing lady.

Mo I know that. But she doesn't. She's a true believer, and she'll die a believer. One of the last things she'll see is your face. You'll hold her hand . . .

Mr Mouse I ain't touchin' no dying kid's hand.

Mo She has to see you before she dies! I can't go back to England and tell them she didn't see you! She can't come here Mr Mouse, she can't be moved. So I'm here to ask you if you'll come to her, in our hotel room.

Mr Mouse She ain't the only one in pain. I hadda' pain for three weeks, an earache pain. Driving me crazy. I had tears in my eyes, and I don't mind admitting it to you lady.

Mo I'm sorry, are you in pain now?

Mr Mouse Had it all day, s'gettin worse.

Mo Have you seen a doctor?

Mr Mouse Yeah. I seen him. Told me I need an operation on my ear. A three thousand dollar operation. Medication extra, then hospital room . . . I ain't got no three thousand dollars. I ain't got three right now, not until I get my pay cheque.

Mo You haven't got medical insurance?

Mr Mouse No, drifted around too much. An' I've always been healthy.

Mo So, what will you do?

Mr Mouse Save some money I guess. Sell my blood. (*Proudly.*) This ain't no socialist country like England. We *pay* for our medicine.

Mo *Laughs.*

Mo England's not a socialist country. It's never been that! And we pay for our medicine. Me and my family bought the wheelchair my daughter spends her days in. We held discos and car boot sales. My husband did a sponsored parachute jump. It put him in bed for a week. God the fairy cakes I've iced over the years! We've turned into full time fund-raisers. We've bought dialysis machines, heart monitors, incubators.

Mr Mouse Thought all that stuff was found for you?

Mo No. Not anymore. My daughter has got cancer of the bones.

Mr Mouse Don't say that word!

Mo I'll give you a hundred and fifty dollars if you'll come with me.

Mr Mouse I ain't goin' near no dying kid, 'specially if she's got . . . that.

Mo Cancer.

Mr Mouse 'Specially that.

Mo She had her photograph in the local paper, 'Brave Angela presents cheque', she collected a hundred and fifty pounds from selling old toys and books. It was mostly old tat, but people were generous. She gave this cheque to the Radiation Department, their cubicle curtains had fallen to pieces and they couldn't afford to replace them. The reporter asked her what her ambition was – kind really because he knew she was terminal. She said, 'I want to go to Orlando to meet Mr Mouse'. It was the landlord in the pub in our village started the fund.

Mr Mouse P'haps I should start a fund, to send me to England, get my ear fixed.

Mo Her hair had fallen out so I bought her a wig. Blonde curls, she loved it. I didn't, she looked like Shirley Temple. A little girl I've never been particularly fond of. (*Pause.*) I'll give you two hundred dollars. We've spent nothing here. She hasn't left the hotel room.

Mr Mouse Why ain't she in hospital?

Mo There's nothing they can do for her, and anyway we couldn't afford it, we've got no insurance. A dying child is a bad risk. A dead cert.

Mr Mouse You don't seem to me like you're bothered too much. You could be lying about this kid, you could be aiming on kidnappin' me once we get outa' here.

Mo Holding Mr Mouse to ransom?

Mr Mouse Happened to Donald Duck once. Students took him, fed him cocaine cake, had him jumpin' in the lake tryin' to paddle like a duck. Ruined his costume. Management laid him off.

Mo This is a photograph of my daughter.

Mo *gives him the photograph.*

Mr Mouse Hell. Bald. Excuse me but she ain't pretty.

Mo This is before.

She hands him another photograph.

Mr Mouse Same kid?

Mo Yes.

Mr Mouse Angela?

Mo Angela Fielding. I'm Maureen Fielding, will you come with me?

Mr Mouse Sorry lady. You see I ain't a person that can do things like that. I don't know what to say or where to put my hands. I ain't good in awkward situations.

Mo But Mr Mouse knows. He's never stuck for a word. He always know what to do. Please.

Mr Mouse Your makin' me feel uncomfortable with myself, and that ain't fair. You see I'm a person who keeps clear of things that ain't nice. I avoid trouble, I live in a clean neighbourhood, don't mind paying extra for it. I don't watch the news on TV and the only films I see are family films. I work here because it's nice. People wave, I wave back, where's the hassle? Leave me alone lady. Go see your daughter, buy her a Mr Mouse puppet.

Mo She's got a Mouse puppet. She's got everything. Bed linen, lamp-shade, rug, stencils, toothbrush, towel, face flannel, mug, cup, plate, bowl, knife, fork, spoon, pencil case, satchel, rucksack, wellingtons, slippers, dressing gown, pyjamas, tee shirts. We've paid for a visit! You owe us a visit! She thinks you're real.

Mr Mouse So blame the Management. I just work here!

Mo You *hide* here, where it's nice, where everybody's happy. The ultimate dream, and you're the star, and cancer and poverty and violence and dirt are outside the gates with all the people who can't afford the entrance ticket.

Mr Mouse So what's wrong with that? You want just anybody to come in. You want it to be *free*?

Mo Yes. Fantasy for all. Free at the point of need. Candy floss and balloons for everyone who needs them.

Mr Mouse Excuse me but you are absolutely crazy. This is an industry, we gotta make money here.

Mo Like selling your blood.

Mr Mouse And sperm, I done that before. An' I been a guinea pig in research labs.

Mo I wouldn't have thought that was 'nice'.

Mr Mouse I made a thousand dollars. I got a clean room, good food. A few headaches, a little nausea, but nothing much else.

Mo Two hundred and fifty dollars.

Mr Mouse I hate death. I seen a dead person.

Mo Angela isn't dead. She's only dying. She's alive. It's such a very simple thing. You go into the room. You wave. You go up to her, you take her hand. You kiss her, you stay there for one minute, she won't ask you any questions, she can't talk. You wave goodbye, you go. Outside the hotel room I, or my husband, give you two hundred and fifty dollars towards your surgery. You go. Simple. Then I go to Angela and give her an injection of morphine alcohol and heroin and she passes away to a place where there's no pain.

Mr Mouse You kill the kid?

Mo Yes.

Mr Mouse You said she was dying.

Mo She is. She's dying in the most terrible agony. I will not allow her to live through another night like last night. Her medication does nothing for her now.

Mr Mouse Wait a minute, if I go, you kill the kid, you're expectin' me to play God.

Mo You are God! Millions worship you. Who's ever seen a picture of *God*? Who could describe *Him*? Catholics worship you. Hindus, Muslims, Protestants, Buddhists, Africans. They adore you, Eskimos, Chinese, you're ever present, almighty, compared to you God's got a walk on part.

Mr Mouse That's a wicked blasphemy. You'll be struck down sure as hell.

Mo Do you think I care if I live or die?

Mr Mouse Yes, I think if it come to it, you'd want to live.

Mo Do you? Thank you. Mr Mouse, I've only got three hundred dollars and that's the truth. Will you come with me for three hundred dollars?

Mr Mouse No.

Mo *sinks to her knees.*

Mo I'm so tired. We don't sleep. She doesn't. It goes on and on and on. Silent screaming, her face pleading to us to help her. And we can't. We can do nothing but watch her and feed her drugs which don't work. Last night her father knocked her out. Hit her on the jaw. She was unconscious for ten minutes. God, did we enjoy that ten minutes! We had a vodka and tonic from the mini-bar. We went into the bedroom and sat on the bed and held hands and drank our drinks. We didn't speak to each other, we waited for her to come round. There was a bruise on her chin.

Mr Mouse He bruised her! That's child abuse, an indictable offence.

Mo (*laughing*) A bruise! My child's body is being eaten away – a bruise is nothing, it's a fly on a mountain. (*Pause.*) Mr Mouse, please come with me, make Angela happy.

Mr Mouse I ain't havin' nothin' to do with killin' a kid.

Mo *lies down on the floor, she faces the audience.*

Mo If I had a gun I'd force you there. I'd poke it in your ribs, I'd frighten you into going.

Mr Mouse Don't lie on the floor, it ain't nice. Pull your skirt down.

Mo I don't suppose I can interest you in sex?

Mr Mouse No.

Mo I small of death don't I? The sickroom travels with me wherever I go. I'll sleep here I think. I can't go back without you. Let me sleep.

Mr Mouse *crosses to* **Mo***, he pulls her up, he supports her while she stands, unsteadily. She is dog tired, he continues holding her.*

Mo Mr Mouse take it all away, make us laugh, amuse us.

Mr Mouse *leads* **Mo** *to the chair, he sits her down. He performs a* **Mr Mouse** *routine. The routine is of* **Mr Mouse** *visiting* **Angela** *in the hotel room. He tiptoes in, his finger to his lips. He tiptoes over to where* **Angela** *is lying, he bends over, he kisses* **Angela***, he then takes* **Angela's** *hand and holds it for twenty seconds. He puts the hand back. He looks down at* **Angela***, he wipes his eyes. He tiptoes away, backwards. He blows a kiss to* **Angela***. He goes out of the imaginary door.*

Mo Yes, that's all you have to do. Oh and we'd like a photograph of you and Angela together. To show the people at home. To prove that their money hasn't been wasted. They raised over five thousand pounds in three months. People are so good. When Angela is dead I'm going to spend my time raising funds for the National Health Service. I shall have nothing else to do that's more important.

Mr Mouse You're a good woman Mrs Fielding.

Mo What do you mean, good?

Mr Mouse Way you care about your daughter. Way you raise money for strangers.

Mo I have no choice but to look after my daughter, and I raise the money because I'm full of rage and hatred. (*Shouting.*) Why her? Why me? What did *she* ever do to deserve her awful life? (*Confiding.*) Mr Mouse, the newspaper called her brave. They call anybody who steps into a hospital brave nowadays. But she isn't brave, she doesn't bear her pain and her suffering with nobility, and why should she? Pain is pain. It's called pain because it's painful, and it hurts. It fills the mind. It reduces us. She's ten years old. Why should she be brave? I could have filled a thousand buckets with the tears she's shed over the past two years. I want her out of it. My husband's got a watch, a good one. Gold, waterproof to a thousand feet. It's a stop-watch, and it's got an alarm and a compass. Three hundred dollars and the watch.

Mr Mouse I can't do it. I'm not a good person like you. I ain't never been a good person, only in my heart. I ain't never put no money in a collectin' tin. I don't agree with that.

Mo We have some political friends. Barbara and Ken Goodwin. They don't agree with fund-raising. They say the government should provide the money, not ordinary people. But then Barbara and Ken are very healthy people, and they haven't been in hospital lately. They haven't seen the nurses stealing cotton wool from other wards. They haven't seen a young doctor falling asleep while he was taking Angela's blood pressure. They haven't seen the queues in the radiation department, (*Shouting.*) because the sodding machine has broken down again! (*Pause.*) Mr Mouse, if you came with us you could do one good thing. You'd feel better about yourself, you'd leave that hotel room a better person.

Mr Mouse Let me figure it through.

Mo Do it for Thomas Harton Wilberforce.

Mr Mouse *shakes his head sadly. He places his hand over his heart. He rubs his eyes.*

Mo I hear what you're telling me. You're sorry for Angela?

Mr Mouse *shakes his head. He points towards* **Mo**. *He rubs his eys.*

Mo You're sorry for *me?*

Mr Mouse *nods. He comes up to* **Mo**. *He strokes her hair. She lays her head on his chest.*

Mo Mr Mouse will you make me happy? That's what you exist for isn't it? To make us happy. To make us laugh.

Mr Mouse *gently pushes* **Mo** *away from him. He starts to do a soft shoe shuffle,* **Mo** *laughs. She holds her hand out to him, he takes it.*

Mr Mouse I gotta get permission, to make a home visit. This is a tough management, Disneyland it ain't.

Mo She'll wait. Thank you Mr Mouse.

True Love Stories

Harwant S Bains

True Love Stories was first performed at the Royal Court Theatre Upstairs on 2 July 1990.

Characters:

Dipti

Meredith

Directed by Lindsay Posner

A spartan interview room in an annexe of the Immigration service at Heathrow Airport. A desk and two chairs, on the desk a collection of thick files. **Meredith,** *an Immigration official, stands over the desk casually sorting through some papers. In one corner stands* **Dipti Pankanya**. *She is dressed in a smart grey suit. A beat, then she steps into the centre of the room.*

Dipti Excuse me, I was told . . .

Meredith Oh, yes, yes please do come in. (*A beat,* **Dipti** *steps towards the desk.*) Mrs . . . (**Dipti** *is silent.*) Mrs Pan . . . How do you say. . .?

Dipti – Pankanya.

Meredith Yes. Of course.

Meredith *sits down, still looking at the file.* **Dipti** *remains standing.*

Meredith Yes. We've had a long chat.

Pause. **Meredith** *looks up.*

Dipti I'm sorry?

Meredith Your husband and I. Please do sit down. (**Dipti** *sits down.* **Meredith** *smiles.*) It's not 'against the rules' after all, though it does help to be on your toes. (*He looks at her. She is uncomprehending.*) Yes. Now what I have here (*He indicates the file.*) is our file on information gathered in the course of various enquiries into this matter.

Dipti This matter?

Meredith Yes.

Dipti What kind of information?

Pause.

Meredith Well, for example I can see from these papers that you are an exceptionally well qualified young woman presently working for a market research organization at middle management level. It's all that kind of thing. (*Smiling.*) Nothing sinister.

Dipti I see. Yes.

Meredith The purpose of this interview is to try and establish certain other relevant facts.

Dipti Yes.

Meredith To establish the truth if you like.

Dipti The truth?

Meredith Perhaps that sounds . . .

Dipti No. You want to know . . .

Meredith – I'm sure you'll appreciate the importance of this process.

Beat.

Dipti . . . Yes.

Meredith As you will know, certain questions have been put to Mr Pan . . . Pankanya regarding the circumstances of your meeting and the subsequent events. (*Pause. He looks at her.*) My job now is to assess his account by asking you to give a similar – um – narrative.

Dipti You want us to prove –

Meredith No, no. It's not a question of proofs. Please don't feel as if you are in some way on trial.

Dipti But the decision is yours.

Beat.

Meredith Yes. At this stage it is. (*Short pause.*) I presume you've received some advice on this matter.

Dipti No.

Meredith I see.

Dipti Not really advice. We spoke briefly to a solicitor.

Meredith Oh, so you did seek advice.

Dipti He couldn't really see any special problem with our case. . . . He did seem very overworked.

Meredith I see.

Dipti To be honest this whole thing surprised me.

Meredith Did it? In what sense?

Dipti Well, we met over here. I mean, I didn't go out of the country or anything. It was a chance thing. A chance meeting. I thought there would be no question about it. I assumed it would be a private matter.

Meredith Well, perhaps that was what you hoped.

Dipti That was what I assumed.

Meredith But let me assure you that there is nothing 'private' in a foreign national – an Indian national in Mr Pankanya's case – arriving in this country ostensibly on holiday and then subsequently seeking leave to remain permanently.

Dipti But we –

Meredith At that point it becomes a matter of National significance.

Dipti Does it? Oh. I see.

Meredith Good, it's important that you do see the rationale behind this process. We, must assess every case within a framework of immigration policy. I'm sure you will agree that we cannot allow a situation to develop whereby people believe that they can assist foreign nationals to gain residence here simply by offering the helping hand of a marriage of convenience. This is why we must become involved.

Dipti Yes.

Meredith We're gatekeepers if you like. (*Smiling.*) Or bouncers if you prefer.

Pause. **Dipti** *glances nervously around the room. She smiles.*

Dipti So. Can we get it over with do you think?

Pause.

Meredith I don't think so.

Dipti Oh.

Meredith No. Not 'get it over with'. That would be . . .

Dipti I see. Yes.

Meredith I didn't finish.

Dipti No. Sorry.

Meredith Look. Lets take a deep breath. Obviously this is difficult for you. (*Pause. He looks at the file and laughs.* **Dipti** *looks concerned.*) I'm nearly twice your age and you earn nearly twice as much as I do. You must be very talented.

Dipti I don't know.

Pause.

Meredith You must let yourself relax. Suspend your suspicions awhile. (*He makes a note in the file.* **Dipti** *watches him nervously.*) This is not something to be rushed. It's far too important a matter. It is – um – desirable that you fully understand.

Dipti Yes.

Meredith For your own sake. (*Pause.*) Otherwise . . . (*Pause.*) We don't want to leave a gulf of, well, of understanding between each other. This is something I explained to your . . . to Mr Pankanya.

Dipti Right.

Short pause.

Meredith He . . . his English isn't quite . . .

Dipti He's learning. It has improved since we first –

Meredith Yes. That is something I would like to examine.

Dipti What?

Meredith When you first met. The circumstances and so on. Perhaps you would like to guide me through the course of events.

Dipti I'll do my best.

Meredith Good. It is important that we have your complete account.

Dipti It's very difficult.

Meredith In what sense? That does seem a strange – um – admission.

He makes a note in the file.

Dipti I only meant in the sense that you don't . . . note things down at the time. I mean you don't expect to have to provide a detailed report later. These things, well at the time they are just part of your normal life. You just carry on through casually without thinking or taking stock of the situation.

Meredith I find in genuine cases there are never too many difficulties.

Dipti Oh. I see.

Meredith Once we get through the initial stages. It's just a question of going through the whole process step by step. You'll surprise yourself at your own ability to recreate things you thought had passed from your mind. I am constantly and pleasantly surprised by the ability of the brain to retain the most slender detail, things unnoticed by the conscious mind which – with the right kind of questioning – emerge to add what is often a vital nuance to the picture we build up.

Pause.

Dipti Well. It sounds like a very interesting job.

Meredith It has it's upside certainly. But my purpose is a serious one I'm afraid. I see a lot of, well, deception for want of a better word.

Dipti I see. That can't be very nice I suppose.

Meredith Nice? No. (*He smiles.*) I used to work at Dover. You wouldn't believe the lengths people would go to. Inside crates, under the false floors of lorries, you name it they tried it.

Pause.

Dipti There is one thing –

Meredith I'll be happy to clarify any detail for you.

Dipti Well, what exactly is it you want to find out about us?

Meredith It's quite simple.

Dipti Really.

Meredith Of course. I merely want to establish the reasons for your entering into this particular marriage. I want to know all the details, all the relevant facts so that I can thereby seek to establish whether the marriage was a legitimate one.

Dipti A legitimate one?

Meredith Yes.

Dipti What does that mean?

Meredith Whether or not the marriage was constituted in order to gain entry for your husband into this country. We call it the 'primary purpose' criteria. It is a difficult matter of course, but you'll appreciate why such a test is necessary.

Dipti No. Not really. I really don't.

Pause.

Meredith I see. Well. (*He stands.*) That really is unfortunate.

Dipti I'm not being funny, but I truly can't see how my decision to marry a particular man . . . well how that can be anybody's business but my own. I can't see where the government comes into it.

Meredith Now that is a problem.

Dipti Is it?

Meredith Yes. This attitude you have. (*Pause. He sits down and makes a note in the file.*) Perhaps I can explain further. (*Pause. He leans back in his chair, his attitude becoming discernibly less formal.*] Well, now look at these arranged marriages for example.

Dipti Yes.

Meredith Marriages without consent.

Dipti That's not very accurate.

Meredith They are 'arranged' after all.

Dipti But almost always with the consent of the people being married. They agree to the process because they regard it as an inherent part of their background. They are always free to walk away. No one chains them to the floor.

Meredith But I'm afraid that to our way of looking at things, I mean the way the English look at it, without love there cannot be a genuine marriage.

Dipti Is the English way of looking at things the only way?

Meredith Of course not. Otherwise the world would be a very boring place wouldn't it. No, I'm all for a touch of variety. But there are certain basic principles which serve as a basis for our traditions, our laws. It is those principles that we uphold.

Dipti So what proportion of English marriages are due to love?

Meredith All of them I would hope.

Dipti What about people who marry for money, or because of a pregnancy, or on a silly whim, or because they need to keep their parents happy so as not to get written out of the will, or for whatever other reason that you can think of. What about those people?

Meredith Yes, there are undoubtedly people like that.

Dipti But they don't have to answer to anyone but themselves.

Meredith No.

Dipti They don't have to reveal intimate personal details to some state official before they can gain permission to live with one another in the same place.

Meredith No. Not if they are both British Citizens.

Dipti But I am a British Citizen. Why don't I have the right to marry anyone I choose for whatever reason I choose to?

Meredith Because this little island we live on can only take on board a certain number of passengers. Otherwise we'll be falling off the edge and into the North Sea.

Dipti I'm not talking about mass immigration, I'm talking about a basic freedom of choice for a British Citizen.

Meredith And I'm trying to explain that your freedoms have to be viewed in terms of the interests of the wider community, of the Nation.

Dipti You know, I read somewhere – um –

Meredith In a newspaper perhaps?

Dipti Sorry?

Meredith In *The Guardian?*

Dipti I can't quite remember where it was. But on average more people emigrate from this Country than immigrate.

Meredith That is the case in some years I suppose.

Dipti It seems to me . . . It seems to a lot of people that your major worry is about letting more black people into the country. I mean people from the EEC can come and go as they please. So on the whole can white Americans and Australians and South Africans.

Meredith You have been doing some research haven't you?

Dipti Not particularly. It's fairly common knowledge in my community. It's something that gets talked about. I must admit that until now I hadn't thought about it at any length. It never seemed particularly relevant to me. But now. Being treated like this.

Meredith – Like what?

Dipti Like some kind of criminal.

Meredith Mrs Pankanya, let me tell you that until now the system has dealt very lightly with you. Your husband has been free to roam the streets. You have been given the opportunity to present your case and receive a fair hearing in accordance with the relevant statute and regulations.

Dipti So I've been lucky? Is that what you're telling me?

Meredith You could put it like that. The fact is that many people in your husband's position would have found themselves in a detention centre pending a hearing. Indeed, that is still an option open to us if we do not feel that we are receiving your fullest cooperation.

Dipti Is that a threat?

Meredith I would not want you to be ignorant of the context within which we are speaking. But it's not in my nature to threaten.

Pause.

Dipti I feel sick.

Pause.

Meredith Would you like some water?

Dipti I was born and brought up in this country. I never thought I'd be made to feel so . . .

Meredith Look, the problem, I mean from our point of view, from the point of view of English people generally, is that though you say this, though you invoke the fact of your birth or your citizenship whenever it serves your interests, there doesn't seem to be a genuine will in your community to take it's proper place within the wider society. I personally think Mr Tebbit put it quite well.

Dipti I don't even like cricket.

Meredith No, it's a man's game I suppose. (*He smiles.*) Perhaps it was a rather facile example he used, but the point was to raise certain issues. About loyalties. I mean, for example, all this hoo-haa by the Moslems. It's a perfect illustration of how so many of your people seem unwilling to adopt any of the basic values of this country.

Dipti I'm not a Moslem.

Meredith No, I realize that. But you see my point?

Dipti So should the Moslems all convert to christianity?

Meredith No. Of course not.

Dipti Then should they not feel offended? Perhaps the reason they are so very angry is because they feel so powerless, so unheard. If you think people can't hear what you say, I think it's a natural instinct to raise your voice, and perhaps you end up shouting louder than you had ever intended.

Meredith You spoke earlier of feeling that your freedoms were being impinged. Well, freedom of speech is a vital liberty.

Dipti Freedom to say anything?

Meredith More or less.

Dipti Then why is it that I remember a couple of years ago voices being raised in protest about a play – I think it was about Zionism – which was going to be put on by a London theatre. It became quite a big issue for a while. Well in the end that play was cancelled wasn't it? I didn't hear many of the people who are condemning the Moslems now raising any great hue and cry over that. If this principle is sacred, and I agree that it is, then it should at the very least be applied evenly to all. You can't help but think it comes down to who is making the protest.

Meredith Well, the circumstances were probably very different.

Dipti It seems to me that the most obvious difference was the fact that the Jewish community has far more of a voice amongst the middle classes, amongst intellectuals and artists and writers and the people who actually go to the theatre or read books than the Moslems who are protesting about the *Satanic Verses* do. Unfortunately for them, they are mostly just ordinary working-class people from rural backgrounds who just don't have any clout. They have no power and they don't speak the language that the powerful in this country speak. There's no possibility of a meaningful dialogue because each side is living in quite a different kind of world. One is a world of privilege and power, the other of prejudice, deprivation and dislocation.

Pause.

Meredith Well . . . *The Mousetrap* was the last play I went to see.

Dipti Oh.

Meredith It was very good. (*Pause.*) There is a problem here isn't there?

He makes a note. Pause.

Dipti We met at my cousin's wedding. That was where I first saw him. He saw me and asked about me. A meeting was organized with the approval of my family. We both liked each another very much. Yes, perhaps we fell in love. We went out together and got to know each another. It was not something I thought would ever happen to me in quite that way. I would not normally have considered a relationship let alone a marriage with a man from India. But the attraction was undeniable. It blossomed. It really did. I have a career. A good job. Nothing was forced on me.

Meredith *has been taking notes.*

Meredith Yes. That more or less tallies with the account given by your husband. (*Short pause.*) But when I spoke of a problem, I was thinking more of the problem that so many of you seem to have in making an appropriate adjustment to life in this country.

Dipti I was born –

Meredith Yes. We're seeing people like you now. The first born. The first of the English-Indians. Or Indian-English.

Dipti So what is my problem?

Meredith Simply that you don't appreciate the sense of loss, the sense of mourning that the English feel for a way of life that has passed us by. We had no say in the matter you see. No specific referendum was taken. The face of this country has been disfigured without any thought for the feelings of the indigenous population. We have been presented with a *fait accompli*, and there are many who feel hurt and anger that this should have happened. Whole areas, whole towns have lost their former identity, they have become unrecognizable. Look at the place you come from – I drive through there at times, it's like Bombay or Calcutta, not West London. I can remember a time not so long ago when that town was just another sleepy suburb.

Dipti I think it's sad you feel that way. Perhaps you just don't like to see change.

Meredith It depends on the nature of the change. I suppose we are by nature a conservative people.

Pause.

Dipti But you could just as easily have felt that this change which you see was a good thing, that some variety had been added to a tiny corner of England, that England has been enriched and it's identity made deeper . . . more complex. I think the kind of England you mourn the passing of, well I think that it was never any more than a place in your heart, maybe something you read in a poem. You see, I don't regard myself as problematic in any way. I don't feel that by being in this country I am encroaching upon anyone else, denying anyone else the right to live in their own ways. The only time I feel the need to respond, to pipe up and say something, is when I feel that people are treading on my toes without just cause.

Meredith *is looking at his notes.*

Meredith One thing you said.

Dipti Yes.

Meredith In your – um – account.

Dipti ?

Meredith You said 'Yes, perhaps we fell in love'.

Dipti Yes.

Meredith 'Perhaps'?

Dipti I'm not sure. Well . . . The term, it seems misplaced in a way.

Meredith So if it was not love, I mean, if it wasn't that first glance across a crowded room, then what was it that pulled you towards this man?

Dipti I think . . . you have to allow for the fact that things work in a slightly different way with us. We don't bandy the 'l' word around in everyday conversation with quite the gay abandon as is the custom here.

Meredith But don't you believe there is such a thing as true love?

Dipti Perhaps there is.

Meredith 'Perhaps' again. I would have thought that love, the possibility of love in all it's various manifestations is the most basic source of our humanity.

Dipti I don't think many of those that use the word have a very clear idea of what it might refer to. I think most people mean 'romance' when they say 'love'. I'm not sure how the word should be used because I'm not convinced that it's particularly meaningful.

Meredith Perhaps because it is not something you have ever experienced.

Dipti I don't know where truth comes into it. I think you mean real – as in real love – but I don't think reality has much of a place within the world of our emotions. I think there we build our own realities according to a certain sense of ourselves, according to the way in which we were brought up. It's too individual a thing – the heart if you like – it's too private for us to apply some set of universal definitions.

Meredith But then psychology would be an impossible science.

Dipti Yes, perhaps it is. Perhaps that is why we need art.

Meredith I'm sure that that is a fine uplifting sentiment Mrs Pankanya, but I do not think that we have got around to addressing the central issue. I am sure that your time is just as precious as mine.

Dipti But I thought that we were addressing the central issue. The central issue seems to be why I have to go through this process at all.

Meredith It is as I explained.

Dipti All you've explained to me is the fact that because some English people – with the clear implication that I do not fully qualify as English – would rather be living in a pre-war rather than a post-war England, I have to be subject to the humiliation of revealing the most personal details of my life to a government official. I think if this is looked at dispassionately, this procedure by which you judge the 'legitimacy' of my marriage, it cannot be regarded as anything less than an outrage.

Meredith 'An outrage.' I see.

Dipti The Tebbits of this Country speak of 'Our' – as if we blackies are some clearly defined single group – reluctant to integrate, to pledge our loyalties, yet we are all the time made to feel unaccepted, alien, resented for our very presence.

Meredith Then perhaps . . . perhaps you should take the hint.

Dipti Sorry?

Meredith Seek sanctuary. Look at the Russian Jews.

Dipti I'm not quite sure what you're saying.

Meredith Well, to bring it down to a specific example, couldn't you just as easily go and live in India with your husband rather than have him come here? I mean, what with all the problems you think you have in this country. Maybe that would be a better choice.

Dipti I don't believe this.

Meredith It's a perfectly valid question.

Pause.

Dipti I've never considered it. England is very much my home.

Meredith But not your husband's.

Dipti No. (*Pause.*) I think it's natural to want to live in a place where the opportunities are greater. Where it's easier to make a career. I think it's the kind of choice most people would make. There's nothing suspect about that.

Meredith It seems you are implying some very unfortunate facts about India.

Dipti I'm just speaking as a person who wants to get on with life and make the best of it. When people emigrate from here to Australia, it doesn't mean that they are rejecting England as somehow unworthy, it usually simply means that they think they can make a better life for themselves over there.

Meredith If people like yourself, professional people, returned to India, it might be that you could help build it up. That might be another way of looking at it.

Dipti Well, maybe you're right. But for me it's not a question of 'return'. When I go to India I'm not much more than a tourist in a strange country.

Meredith Really.

Beat.

Dipti Maybe that's what you think.

Meredith What?

Dipti That we should all 'go back' as they say.

Pause.

Meredith Well, of course it's not as simple as that. I do think that there is a case to be made for providing encouragement for people who might want to return to the land of their origin. It could be argued that this country should provide comprehensive aid to the former colonies as a way of facilitating the absorbtion of returning immigrants. You see, the situation we have here today is the consequence of Britain having once been an imperial power. We need to begin to untangle ourselves from that history. This is an age when all over Europe nations are re-discovering their identity and asserting their right to – well – to self definition and freedom from foreign influence. I do not see why if the majority desire the maintenance of their separate identity, their Englishness, why that should be a bad thing. Do you understand what I'm trying to say? This is not in some way directed against your community, I think you have just as much right to assert your own identity, but it is probable that these two quite separate ways of living, one born in the East the other in the West, cannot live side by side without conflict. And if I am right about that –

which I think I am – then it is only correct that the minority, the newcomers, should be the ones to, well, pack up and move.

Dipti What about the West Indian community. They aren't 'of the East' are they? Even their language is the same.

Meredith I wouldn't say that. No, I think that their culture is quite distinct. They have very severe problems in this country. I think ultimately the problem is the same.

Dipti It seems to me that if what you say is right, then the world is very soon going to become a very unpleasant place. I mean if people congregate into tightly defined and mutually exclusive groups, that can only be a formula for mutual mistrust and eventual conflict. Surely we should be trying to transcend that.

Meredith Perhaps. But I don't think many would agree with you. It seems to me that perhaps those 'rivers of blood' are an inevitable consequence of any attempt to impose, to graft a foreign, distinct, alien culture upon an indigenous population.

Dipti So is that the justification for the brutalities, the atrocities that black people in this country are subjected to?

Meredith Atrocities? I think you're perhaps getting slightly carried away Mrs Pankanya.

Dipti I have a friend, an old schoolfriend, who lives in a block of council flats with her daughter. On four occasions she has had paraffin poured through her letterbox followed by lighted matches. She's been lucky until now. Her other unofficial mail has included dead rats, human excrement, and letters containing racial abuse and the occasional razor blade.

Meredith That is a terrible thing. But there are these criminal elements, vandals and such like.

Dipti We live with the constant possibility of being picked out and abused and assaulted in almost any situation, from a council estate to a posh restaurant, and for no other reason than the fact that we wear a certain kind of skin. People are beaten, many are murdered for no better reason.

Meredith I would not attempt for a moment to justify the things you speak of. But as I said, it does seem to me that this is an inevitable – though very unpleasant – consequence of a culture, the English or British culture in this case, feeling itself being swamped. People do begin to lash out.

Dipti So what is the 'proper' English culture?

Meredith That is a complex question.

Dipti I mean is it the Northern or the Southern, Welsh or Scottish, Northern Irish? Where are the 'real' English or the 'real' British?

Meredith They are in all those places.

Dipti Are they all the same?

Meredith No. But they are bound together by a common history.

Dipti History. I thought you wanted to untangle yourself from that as far as the blacks go.

Meredith I won't deny that the English are diverse, but it is a diversity within certain confines.

Dipti Do you mean the confines of race?

Short pause.

Meredith Ultimately, yes. However that does not mean I think that to be white is to be superior, simply that it is to be different. I don't think we should be ashamed of wanting to maintain our difference. As I pointed out to you earlier, that is just what your own community wishes to do. (*He looks down at the file.*) We've rather strayed off the point haven't we.

Dipti Yes. We have.

Meredith I think I have enough information.

Dipti Don't you find these views . . .

Meredith Go on.

Dipti Your views. Don't they get in the way. I mean given the work that you are doing.

Meredith My 'views' as you call them are a personal affair. I was perhaps wrong to discuss them. But you seem an intelligent woman. I don't think a frank exchange of attitudes and perceptions can ever be of any harm. As far as my work goes, I simply apply the relevant regulations with as much objectivity as is possible.

Dipti But you have, well . . .

Meredith Discretion?

Dipti Yes.

Meredith To a certain extent. I tend to always err on the side of caution. If my decision is wrong, there is the possibility of an appeal, though their success is very limited. (*Pause.*) You will be informed of the decision on your case in due course.

Dipti Sorry?

Meredith The decision on your case.

Dipti Oh. When will we know?

Meredith In due course.

Dipti Oh. I see. You can't give me any idea of . . .

Meredith I'm afraid not. Thank you so much for your time.

Short pause.

Dipti Yes. Well . . .

She stands.

Meredith Perhaps we have both, well, learned a little.

Dipti *looks at him blankly. The lights go down.*

Goodnight Siobhan

Jeananne Crowley

With many thanks to Eamon Dunphy
without whose help this could not have been written

Goodnight Siobhan was first performed at the Royal Court on 2 July 1990.

Characters:

Siobhan

Cathal

Directed by John Dove

Lights fade up to noise of party/bar somewhere in the distance. We're in a hotel bedroom, behind the door hang 'Make up the room' and 'Do not disturb' signs. There is a bed, chair, door off to bathroom. Minibar, TV and newspapers/briefcase, the paraphernalia of someone away at a conference of some denomination.

Voices of man and woman coming along corridor. (Improvise 'Your place or mine?' stuff.) Hear the doorkey in lock lots of giggles and into the room come **Cathal** *and* **Siobhan**.

Cathal *is a little bit pissed, in good form as we say. Looks between 30 or 40 years of age . . . journalist I'd say though it's not specified. Dubliner, attractive, verbal occasionally verbose, enjoys life to the full . . . given to quoting reams of poetry at the slightest opportunity, not in the least bit arrogant. His ease masks a passionate heart . . . hates violence. Bit of a gent too where the ladies are concerned, though he thinks he's in for a Good Night.*

Siobhan *is Northern Irish ghetto Catholic, raised out of it thanks to British Educational System, University etc., works now in some civil service or* P.R. *capacity. Very attractive, wry, sardonic, nervy but quite, quite self-assured.*

She I'm uh dying for a pee. Won't be a minute . . . just help yourself.

He Where's the ice-bucket?

She (*from bathroom*) What?

He (*as he looks about*) Didn't I tell you? Don't go up to ladies rooms anymore these days unless there's champagne . . . I mean (*Half to himself.*) its the least you could provide if you're intending to seduce me.

She Don't count your chickens pet.

He Well what's it to be? (*During following* **He**'s *at the room's mini-bar muttering about prices or whatever.*) And if you're thinking of having more than one and I love a forward planner, the only thing there's more than one of is whiskey.

She Fine.

He Scotch or Irish . . . need I ask?

She (*still in bathroom but during his next speech in her own time comes out, kicks off her shoes, takes her drink from him and sits feet up on the bed*) I prefer Scotch actually when there's a choice.

He (*laughing to himself at first then getting into telling her the story*) The Europa . . . I used to spend God knows how many . . . weeks at a time here between bombings . . . funny . . . well no of course it's not funny not funny in the least . . . let me tell you about George Best and the Europa . . . he arrived with his girlfriend of the moment, Mary Stavin, Miss World. Asked to Belfast to open two betting shops, getting paid three grand apiece . . . in readies naturally . . . arrives late at night, porter brings them up to the room, of course at this stage everyone in Belfast knows about 'poor wee George' his life all over the tabloids . . . skid row (the stuff of tabloid editors' dreams) . . . anyway porter leaves cases down and George says 'Can you get me a bottle of champagne.' Certainly sir and off he goes. While he's away George takes the six grand out of his pockets, he's got it all in readies, throws it on the bed. Stavin starts taking her gear off, she's sitting there doing her hair in her silk underwear. Knock on the door little guy walks in with the champagne, George signs, says 'beside the bed' he clocks your woman and George gives him a £20 note and just as he backs to the door he says 'Mr Best do you mind if I ask you a question?' 'No problem'. 'It's very personal Mr Best.' 'Fire ahead.' 'Mr Best, where did it all go wrong?'

He'*s enjoyed telling this and laughs at the end.*

He . . . There he was alone with Miss World . . . the bed covered in money and yer man says 'George where did it all go wrong?'

She I used to feel for that poor wee fella, couldn't handle himself . . . that's the problem. Take them out of the ghetto show them the world and they can't handle it. Van Morrison the same, and Higgins how's he for a born again loser. And look at you coming over all sentimental about him. AAAhhh poor wee George! He was only a fuckin' footballer.

He You're all heart Siobhan.

She No room for sentiment where I come from.

He I like that.

She You do?

He Yeh. I like a woman with opinions, a woman who knows what she's about.

She Well thank you!

He Don't mention it.

She I suppose you think I've got my own johnnies in the bag there with maybe a couple of packets spare that you could take back with you to the Free State. Like taking Levi's to Moscow you could make a fortune.

He (*after an amused very slightly pissed pause*) No.

She What?

He (*to himself*) No I won't.

She What?

He I was just considering whether or not to shatter one of your precious little illusions about our glorious Republic but ever mindful of *Time's wingéd chariot* I decided not to because if I even start to begin we'll be here all night.

She I thought that's what you wanted.

He I was hoping for a silent communion, a celebratory pagan ritual, a communiqué without words, beginning *O fair One at thy feet.*

She Catch yourself on!

He *moving towards her feet, received pronunciation as* **He** *pays his respects to one of her feet.*

       Had we but world enough and Time . . .
       This coyness lady were no crime

She *a bit amused, a bit nervy,* **He's** *playful.*

       An Hundred Years should go to praise
       Thine eyes and on thy forehead gaze.
       Two hundred to adorn each breast.
       But thirty thousand to the rest . . .

She What's with the voice?

He You don't like my voice?

She It's not actually my favourite accent.

He What?

She You're sounding very British all of a sudden.

He Oy Veh! Here I am alone with a Beeautiful woman attempting to woo her with one of the sexiest sonnets in the English language . . . you're not telling me you'd prefer Danny Boy, are you?

She I like Danny Boy, what's wrong with Danny Boy?

He Haven't you heard?

He What?

He I hate to be the one to break it to you but . . . Danny Boy is dead. He is no more. Over. Caput. Finis. *Requiescat in pace.* Amen.

She Is he now?

He 'Fraid so and I'll let you into another little secret, we don't dance at the cross-roads anymore either. Actually between you me and the four walls we never did. The late great De Valera's vision of comely maidens and athletic young men forging a pure innocent Eire Nua between the jigs and the reels was only ever a figment of his limited imagination. (*In a rural voice.*) I know what you think, at least I know what I think you think, that we're all decent, Godfearing people living a state of Holy Terror who stroll off to watch the hurling of a Sunday after Mass with our Fainnes and our Pioneer Pins glistening in the sun . . . a song in our hearts and the Proclamation on our lips: (*Mockingly.*)
> 'IRISHMEN AND IRISHWOMEN
> In the Name Of God and Of the
> Dead Generations, Ireland through us
> summons her children to her Flag and
> Strikes for her FREEDOM'

Shall I tell you something? Not a lot of people know this . . . on that fateful Easter Monday when Pearse and the rest of the lads grabbed the General Post Office and loudly declared war on Britain, the good citizens of Dublin on their way, quite properly, to the races at Fairyhouse, spat on those heroes and told them in no uncertain terms to piss off! 'WHAT THE FUCK ARE YOU EEJITS DOING TO OUR POST OFFICE!' And I'm with them. I've had it with Danny Boy. I'm up to here with Danny Boy. Brin Go Brea, the Dark Rosaleen, Chuchaig An Lá, not to mention Wolfe Tone, the Sean Bean Bocht and (**He** *breaks into song.*) 'The Men Behind The Wire!'

She (*mock applause*) Very funny. Very funny.

He I think it's funny, isn't it . . . funny?

She It's getting late.

He What's the matter?

She Nothing.

He Come on. No don't tell me, it was something I said, was it something I said?

She Funnily enough yes but we won't go into all that. Don't get me wrong, I mean you're great crack, a laugh a minute but if you stay well let's just say I don't think it's going to turn out to be the kind of night I need or you want.

He Can I finish my drink . . .

She *doesn't say yes or no.* **He** *picks up his glass, takes a sip and very quietly begins to sing.*

> Oh Danny Boy, the pipes, the pipes are calling,
> From glen to glen and down the mountainside.

The Londonderry Air . . . just for you. (*He blows her a kiss.*)

She Derry, if you please.

He Are you trying to tell me something?

She There is wire you know and there are men behind it.

Softly, **He** *begins to sing again, this time a verse from 'Kevin Barry'.* **He** *finishes the verse and waits.*

He

> Just before he faced the hangman
> In his dreary prison cell
> British soldiers tortured Barry
> Just because he would not tell
> The names of his brave comrades
> And the things they wished to know
> 'Turn informer or we'll kill you'

Kevin Barry answered 'No'.

Pause.

She You've got a lovely voice Cathal.

He But? (*Pause.*) There is a 'But' isn't there?

She Not at all. Whatever gave you that idea?

He Oh just something you didn't say.

She (*wry smile*) You're a bit of a lad really aren't you?

He (*grinning back, sings again*)

> My name is O'Hanlon,
> And I've just turned sixteen.
> My home it is Monaghan
> 'Tis there I was weaned.
> And I've learned all my life
> Cruel England to blame
> And that's why I'm part of . . . The Patriot Game

and what a load of shit that is!

She A load of shit, that's your considered opinion is it?

He Come on, I thought you'd be above all that, a smart girl like you.

She Some of us can't afford to be above it.

He Cruel England to blame? How can I blame England, what have I to blame it FOR? The lovely Georgian city I have the pleasure of living in, the city they built and our gombeen men are hell bent on destroying in the name of progress? For the papers I read, the games I play, the language we're speaking, language that gave me some of the most beautiful poetry ever written . . .

> Wine comes in at the mouth,
> That's all we shall know for truth
> Before we age and die
> I lift the glass unto my mouth
> And look at you and sigh . . .

is poor old England to blame for Yeats and the fact I can now buy my Y-fronts in Marks and Spencer. God bless St Michael, your only man!

She You're deliberately misunderstanding me. I'm not talking about language or literature, art or architecture – I'm talking about men who died, who laid down their lives for your freedom to buy your underwear wherever the fuck you like – men you seem to find it easy to sneer at, well let me tell you I don't. They gave you Yeats and what did they give me? Fuckin' Ian Paisley.

He Now now Siobhan, let's not get all sectarian about this. I tread softly . . . nobody's perfect. Yeats was a Prod too you know . . . 'and I being poor have only my dreams . . . I have spread my dreams under your feet, tread softly for you tread upon my dreams . . .'

She Jesus that's all it is to you, songs and poetry, poetry and song. Have you any notion of what it's like out here in the real world? British soldiers on every street corner, guns and drums, drums and guns. I grew up to the poetry of gunfire and the song of boots kicking the door in at four o'clock on a Sunday morning. So maybe you'll forgive me if I can't find it in my heart to share your love of all things British.

He You're British.

She I'm Irish.

He No no no no no I'm Irish, officially actually you're British. What does it say on your passport?

She Mind your own business.

He Ah Hah! It says United Kingdom doesn't it?

She I have both. I'm entitled to both. I want all my entitlements.

He British AND Irish, I'd say you're confused.

She Not half as confused as you. At least I know where I'm coming from. This IS Ireland, this is not anywhere else and Ireland has got the history it has and what you don't seem to realize is that there's a war going on in your very own country, a war that, whether you like it or not involves you.

He No no no not my country, your country. I am a fully-fledged paid up member of the Republic of Ireland, Eire to be precise. How do I know this? We have our very own entry in the Eurovision Song Contest and our own desk at the UN. Our football team qualified for the World Cup and when we win an Oscar, an Emmy, a Grammy, and the British try and say it's theirs, we know it's not but we're able to forgive them anyway because, poor things, they have so little to celebrate these days. In other words Princess, Northern Ireland is not my country, it's yours and believe me you're welcome to it.

She Pathetic, that's what it is. The feeble attempts of the South of Ireland, especially the middle-classes, of which I take it, you are also a fully-fledged paid up member – to find some way, any way, of celebrating yourselves that is non-political. Look at you, desperate to find something, anything, to make youse feel good about yourselves. What do you need symbols for? It doesn't happen in self-confident countries, countries that can define their own fucking borders.

He We're not celebrating symbols, we're celebrating achievement and calm down would you?

She If you had any real political identity, any sense of who you really are there'd be no need for all this hysteria over a stupid soccer team, or *My Left Foot* or the bloody Tour de France not to mention U2! Imagine attempting to celebrate your national identity through a fuckin' rock and roll band! Bestowing the 'Freedom of the City' on Bob Geldof! Jesus it's a wonder youse don't lay on a welcoming committee for the roadies. 'Welcome home boys and didn't you do well to lug all that heavy gear right round the world. We're proud of you, right on!'

He Hey you're getting very het up over all this. What does it matter to you what we celebrate? As long as we're having a good time. At least we're celebrating, not whingeing, but celebrating ourselves, our nationality, our Irishness. 'And when my Nation takes her place among the Nations of the World, then and only then, let my epitaph be written' . . . I think young Emmet's instructions from the scaffold can safely be said to have been carried out.

She responds with disdain.

He I know, I know things are different in the North of Ireland but all the same . . .

She (*interrupts*) The Six Counties, please.

He Let's compromise and call it Ulster OK?

She No. We won't. Your Constitution says that the six counties belong with the rest of Ireland, all I'm doing is agreeing with it.

He Yeah and it also says a woman's place is in the home, can't have

Dev's notion of rural Utopia dented by the sight of comely maidens going to work in trousers now can we? Come on, its only words. Words, words, words. You can rub them out you know and write in nice new ones. It's not a tablet of stone. Don't tell me your lot are killing people in the name of our Glorious Constitution!

Pause.

She Who said anything about killing people?

He Oh sorry . . . I didn't mean to suggest . . . that you well . . . sorry.

She Anyhow you can call it anything you like, it won't change the fact that Belfast is only one hundred miles up the road from your nice Georgian city with its literary tradition and its wall to wall shopping malls –

He No, I suppose it won't.

She And if you people think you can cut yourselves off from that fact and grow into a separate stream in history that will just flow gently majestically on for evermore then you're talking fuckin' fantasy. You are part of us and we are part of you, we're not going to go away.

He I suppose a fuck is out of the question.

She What?

He Well if I'm part of you and you're part of me, why don't we consummate the relationship here and now? Come on . . . ascend from the metaphorical to the Divine . . . Having both world enough and time . . . this coupling Lady is no crime.

She Jesus Christ is there nothing you take seriously?

He I take you seriously. I'm seriously asking you to take all your clothes off, one at a time, or better still, I'll take them off for you then I'll turn out the light, seriously, take you in my arms and we'll get down to some serious love-making and when it's over, if we've the strength we can have a serious meaningful conversation about the Northern Ireland conflict and what it means to be at cross purposes on this divided island off an island off the coast of Europe. What do you say?

She Finish the foreplay afterwards you mean?

He What?

She Well it seems to me we are in the middle of what I think is a serious conversation already and I wouldn't mind getting a few things clear before deciding whether we've enough in common for me to be able to forget myself in the arms of a man who treats the political history of his country as some kind of joke.

He You're very aggressive.

She No I'm not aggressive. Really I'm not.

He All right you're not. But you sound it. No wonder everybody out there thinks we're all completely cracked.

She What do you mean?

He Out there. The places on the perfume bottles. London Paris New York, the inhabitants of which are convinced that the Emerald Isle is a country full of aggressive See-Here-You gun-toting lunatics. And can you blame them? It's all they ever see faithfully, religiously, reported in the newspapers, radio, TV. Of course they should be smart enough to differentiate between your lot and mine but they're not, they think we're all cut from the same weary bloodstained cloth and naturally I resent it.

She You do?

He Of course I do, wouldn't you? I swear to God I'm not a 'Papist'!

She That's not the impression I get.

He Isn't it?

She Certainly not. Look at your cardinal's funeral with anybody who was anybody at all in the South flocking up to the cathedral to pay their last respects.

He The Carmelite with the Armalite God rest him. Yes, disgusting wasn't it? All the deathly splendour and the lads . . . the two likely lads up there with the best, partaking of Holy Communion in the Name of the Lord. Amen. (*He sings the Amen in Catholic liturgical fashion.*)

She Gerry Adams and Martin McGuinness . . . if that's who you happen to be referring to . . . actually represent a rather large percentage of Catholics in the North and they had tickets you know. Didn't get those from ticket touts. They were invited, properly invited, by the Catholic Hierarchy of your Republic.

He Yeah. Bad 'cess to them. Lucky no one over the age of reason has any faith in that lot any more. Of course, the Age of Reason dawns fairly

randomly down South . . . but the point, the only point, I want to make
is that I AM NOT a dogmatic, intransigent Brit-hating, rabid Republican,
armalite in one hand, ballot-box in the other. Look at me . . .

She *doesn't look at him.*

He (*gently*) Ah come on won't you look at me, just a little peep??

She *looks and maybe even smiles a little.*

He (*teasing accent maybe American*) I'm just a regular guy with a huge
mortgage, a peaceful fucker wouldn't hurt a fly. (*Pause.*) You really have
the most beautiful hair.

She I have?

He
    I heard an old religious man
    But yesternight declare
    That only God above my dear
    Could love you for yourself alone
    And not your yellow hair . . .

She I love that.

He So do I.

She Not the poetry, sunshine, which is merely a convenient distraction
from what you're really saying about me.

He And what's that?

She You're really saying I'm crazy, that people in the North are all mad,
that the whole fuckin' thing is irrational, that no reasonable civilized
person would ever want anything to do with us.

He Yep that's a more or less reasonable résumé of my position.

She The implication being that there is a Solution To The Problem that
we are either too pig-headed, or stupid, or psychopathic or brutalized to
see.

He Right.

She There is another conclusion to be drawn, a more obvious one.

He Tell me.

She That there is no solution to the problem as it stands. You can't reform the Northern state given the way it was set up. 'A Protestant State for a Protestant People' . . . an Ulster Identity like an Ulster Fry is a distinctly Protestant thing. How can Catholics relate to it? How can we accept its police force, respect its judiciary, be loyal to its institutions? What do you want us to do! Trust those nasty wee Prods are going to be nice to us all from now not treat us as second class citizens anymore?

He Why not give it a lash Jack?

She (*with great dry cynicism*) Have faith in their natural goodness you mean? There is no evidence over the past ten, twenty, fifty years that would encourage me to trust them. There's no way any Catholic could do it not within the confines of the Six Counties. The border has got to go.

He Says who?

She Your Government for one. Fianna Fáil. Soldiers of Destiny.

He Pleeease! You're taking History . . . they don't give a tinker's curse anymore. Oh yeah publicly they play the game, make all the right noises and sure why wouldn't they? The aul' green card can be very useful betimes when there are votes to be got in the remoter regions of our green and peasant land, but privately, and I'm sorry if it hurts, none of us down there care any more. You're costing us a fortune. We just don't give a shit! Why should it be our responsibility. Sort it out amongst yourselves.

She It's not your responsibility. It's your fuckin' Destiny.

He No fuckin' way.

She History has imposed this upon you and I'm terribly sorry if it interferes with the Good Life you imagine you're having and can continue to have without us. But the truth, the one single truth tens of thousands of Catholics have had to learn over the past twenty years, and it wasn't easy, is that there is no way for us to express ourselves . . . of even beginning to understand our identity as Irish Catholic people other than in the context of this whole island.

He *having had an idea that amuses him, and it's the last* **He** *will try to get through on this level.*

He What about you?

She What about me?

He Do you think you could demonstrate the truth of this abstract proposition?

She What?

He Identity is only a word . . . a selection of syllables gathered together in order to describe a concept which in itself is abstract . . . right?

She (*suspicious*) Yes . . .

He And obviously *real* expression of one's identity can never occur in the abstract.

She So?

He (*big grin*) So why don't you and I get down and *really* express our separate identities in the context of this bed? And in the process forge a living metaphor of the Good Life that you imagine is going on down South without you!

She Jesus, you're so sharp you'll cut yourself.

He It's up to you of course, I've no desire to force Union upon you.

She I've got a feeling, and it's only a feeling mind, correct me if I'm wrong, that you don't take anything I say seriously at all.

He What am I supposed to say to that Princess?

She Don't call me Princess.

He I'll take you as seriously as you'll let me. I just don't believe all 'personal interaction' has to take the form of political debate. (*Sighs.*) Can't you forget yourself for an hour or so? Forget all about where you're coming from and Be in the Now (**He** *smiles.*) . . . I can tell you're too young to remember flower power, Zen and the Art of Motor Cycle Maintenance. (*Sings.*) All you need is love? Such a pity, such a waste, (*And lifting his glass.*) such a shame.

Pause.

She Do you know why I asked you up here tonight?

He You couldn't wait to get your hands on my body.

She I thought you might be a fellow-traveller.

He And now you're disappointed. I don't share your politics ergo I can't share your bed. Is that it?

She Something like that yes.

He (*tired and truthful both*) Much as I'd like to fake it – I can't. 'Too fast to live . . . too old to lie.' I can't get carried away on waves of meaningless rhetoric just so as you can feel good about yourself and what you're doing in the name of a United Ireland. The TRUTH is it disgusts me. In fact, as far as I'm concerned, you can tow Northern Ireland into the middle of the Atlantic and sink it. I've had enough. Genug already.

She *ignoring the personal implications and trying to keep up the level of political argument but she is hurt.*

'Tow Northern Ireland into the Atlantic?' Well, I suppose it's not a bad image, as images go, but it's not going to happen. Instead of walking round with your eyes shut, why not open them and take a good look at what not giving a fuck about us really means!

He (*weary*) Why does it have to 'mean' anything?

She Because the conflict isn't going to stop just because you can't be doing with it. The conflict is going to continue to spill across the border and life in the South is going to be increasingly poisoned for as long as you try to keep a lid on it. If you think you're going to betray us by cutting yourselves off and conveniently pretending we don't exist, well you're going to have to learn different. It effects everyone on this Island of OURS, you included.

He (*genuinely angry for the first time*) It's not fucking OURS, its Theirs as well. You haven't got the Right to bomb, maim and murder a million Protestants into something they don't belong to and never did. Whatever happened in the past. Whatever you think 'they' did to you. However many jobs you were kept out of, however cold your little outdoor lav was on a winter's night. Did your Mammy never tell you, two wrongs don't make a right? Don't get me wrong you had my sympathy once . . . long ago on a Civil Rights march in Derry but your, your awful . . . awesome capacity for violence . . . put an end to all that.

She Oh I see. As long as it was a children's crusade, St Joan in a mini-skirt and lots of revolutionary punters marching up and down asking nicely for Democracy please, it was all OK. Is that it?

He Yes.

She Armies have guns, policemen have guns, why shouldn't the Falls Road have guns? Why shouldn't the Bogside have guns? Why should everybody else but us have guns? What are we? Different? If you come from the Bogside.

He I don't.

She Well I do and if you come from where I'm coming from you cannot afford to accept the notion that the State has a legitimate monopoly on the use of violence.

He And we're supposed to join in are we? Go back to hating the British whom we've forgiven long ago, and in the name of something as out of date as the fuckin' Proclamation? And if we don't, you'll just take over and do it in our name. You're not Irish not the way I am, you've forfeited your claim.

She All we're doing is finishing off what 1916 began, for the bit youse conveniently left behind.

He That's where you're stuck isn't it? In a fuckin' time-warp. Surprise, surprise, there's been some progress since then and I'll tell you what it is. Pearse, our greatly venerated Republican hero was wrong, all wrong 'We may make mistakes in the beginning and shoot the wrong people but bloodshed is a cleansing, sanctifying thing.' Oh, the man was seriously disturbed. A blithering idiot Connolly called him. We finally figured it out all by ourselves. It doesn't work. Violence, bitterness, revenge are a waste of time. So, we gave 'em up, turned away from the Past and with it threw out the béal bocht, down-trodden, lamentable eejity excuse for human beings we used to be. We stopped feeling sorry for ourselves, stopped blaming other people for all our misfortunes. And if you do that, if you take a vote for Life, you find you don't have the stomach for Death anymore. Killing doesn't work. Government Warning, it's bad for your health. We want nothing more to do with it. Step by bloody step you lost us. Do you need to hear how?

She Go on don't let me interrupt your flow.

He Birmingham, Guildford, The Droppin' Well. Bloody Friday the day the bus station was bombed into little bits of people, bits that were picked up limb by limb and put into little plastic bags . . . Hyde Park 'a Legitimate Military Target???' Men, armed to the teeth with slide trombones . . . and that Sunday, that November Sunday. An ordinary decent man holding his daughter's hand as her young life bled away beneath a pile of rubble.

She Spare ME the emotion sweetheart. All armed struggles are nasty. By their nature violent and nasty and unpleasant. People who say the IRA should fight a cleaner war are allowing themselves a luxury which is not available to the people actually carrying out the struggle, people who have to fight with their backs to the wall. This IS no way of doing that without the risk of all these horrors. So it's not a question of saying that they shouldn't have bombed Harrods or they 'shouldn't be shooting unarmed UDR men' the question is: How do you end it?

He Nail the lie.

She What?

He Nail the lie! Stop pretending you're locked in mortal combat with the Military Might of British Imperialist Repression and tell the truth.

She What Truth?

He (*leaning forward conspiratorially*) The Terrible Truth.

She Which is?

He That you can't, won't, get on with your neighbours. Your real live actual Protestant neighbours. People who shop in the same shops as you, who use the same swimming-pools, borrow books from the same libraries – who breathe the same air – people who buy their underwear in Marks & Spencer too. You won't ever forgive them will you? Isn't the reality that you have to win? That for you it's not a problem, it's a conflict? Someone's going to lose, someone's going to have to lie down and it ain't gonna be the Croppies! And anytime the slightest sign of life emerges you blow it to smithereens.

She The Catholic Community would accept in the morning a solution that would give them equal citizenship, a real sense of being fully equal participants in civic life. There's absolutely do doubt that if that were presented to us in the morning, support for the IRA would diminish very quickly indeed.

He Oh yeah?

She Yes. Nobody wants this thing to continue. How could they? It's not a lack of will!

He Prove it.

She I don't have to prove it.

He (*stretching with a yawn*) Yes you do. Stop moving the goalposts and put out your hand. (*He gets up.*) Confucius he say . . . A journey of a thousand miles begins with one step . . . take it.

She Where are you going?

He To bed.

She You can stay if you want to.

He I haven't got it in me. Sorry. It was nice meeting you . . . we must get together sometime.

She Wait.

He What is it?

She I just want to say . . . (*Pause.*) I'm not . . . I . . .

There's a small silence between them.

He (*at the door*) You know sometimes I wonder whether we might not all have been better off leaving the pillar-boxes red and standing up for God Save The Queen . . . (*Smiles.*) . . . ssshhh but don't ever tell anyone I said that! I'd be shot!

She I won't.

He Goodnight.

She Goodnight.

He leaves and she sits silent, sad and silent . . . upset and then from her bag or wherever takes the two passports and flings them from her angry, sad, frustrated and, ultimately alone.

Fade up music. The last verse of A Song for Ireland *sung by Mary Black.*

Blackout.